Penguin Handbook PH76

House Maintenance and Repairs

G. C. A. Tanner spent his early childhood in China and then lived in Australia. After leaving school he worked for a short time in a country town in New South Wales as a sort of office boy, first at a service station, then for a manufacturer of fibrous plaster, and finally for an architect. Influenced by these last two experiences, he studied architecture at the University of New South Wales, where he received an honours diploma, and then worked in architects' offices in Sydney and in the north of England until he came to London in 1958. He is now on the editorial staff of the *Architect's Journal*.

G. C. A. Tanner married an architect whilst they were both students, and he and his wife, small son, and delinquent black cat live in a tall, late Georgian terrace house. Consequently he is irrevocably involved in house improvements, maintenance, and repairs.

G. C. A. Tanner

House Maintenance and Repairs

Penguin Books

Penguin Books Ltd, Harmondsworth,
Middlesex, England
Penguin Books Inc., 3300 Clipper Mill Road,
Baltimore 11, Md, U.S.A.
Penguin Books Pty Ltd, Ringwood,
Victoria, Australia

First published 1965

Made and printed in Great Britain by
Cox and Wyman, Ltd, London, Reading, and
Fakenham

Set in Monotype Times

Contents

Acknowledgements

The author wishes to thank T. A. Baker, J. B. Screeton, S. Froud, and the technical officers of the British Electrical Development Association, the Coal Utilization Council, Esso Petroleum Company Limited, and the Gas Council, who read and commented upon certain chapters. He is particularly indebted to Peter Burberry and Donald Foster who each read a number of chapters and offered helpful criticism and much encouragement. Betty Burberry read some of the chapters and her comments, as those of a layman, were most useful. Thanks are also due to Jean Saunders who undertook the onerous task of typing a good part of the text. The author received consistent encouragement from his wife, who brought to bear the critical eye of the housewife as well as the technical knowledge of the architect.

The table on page 164 is reproduced from the *Esso Guide to House Heating*. The chart on page 161 is reproduced from *Domestic Heating*, edited by W. B. F. Shaw, published by Temple Press Books Ltd.

CHAPTER 1

Introduction

The varieties of do-it-yourself enthusiasts range from those who will go so far as to mend a fuse and no further to those who, given the opportunity, would probably not baulk at building their own houses. It seems reasonable, therefore, to begin by stating specifically what this book sets out to do and for whom it is intended.

The purpose of the book is first to describe in as simple and non-technical a way as possible the details of house-construction, and then to show what parts need regular maintenance, how often they need it, what it involves, what parts are likely to go wrong, and how they should be repaired. It is aimed primarily at the interested amateur with a little basic knowledge and considerable enthusiasm. The book describes how to do those jobs of mainten-ance and repair around the house which he (or she) should feel capable of doing. But it would be incomplete if it stopped short at this. If the reader cannot or does not choose to carry out these jobs himself he has to get somebody else, a professional, to do them. Where, therefore, it is felt that a task is beyond the amateur it is described in just enough detail to give him the knowledge and confidence to instruct his builder as to what he wants done and, when it is done, to see that he has got what he asked for. At times the distinction may seem arbitrary but lack of detail at any point is unlikely to deter the exceptionally enthusiastic and skilful.

No matter how enthusiastic or knowledgeable the amateur, however, from time to time he is likely to need technical or pro-fessional advice. Appendices 1 and 2 on pages 209 and 210 list organizations and services available to help him.

*

The enormous amount of building taking place today must be apparent to the most casual observer. Over the last ten years or so there have been far-reaching developments in new building materi-als and techniques stimulated by the demand for more and more buildings – more schools, more hospitals, more houses. But, if the ways of building change and improve, the purpose served by the structure of a building does not. Although the post-war house has enjoyed its share of new materials (aluminium gutters and down-pipes, polythene water pipes, plastic floor finishes, for example) its structure has not altered substantially since the last century when the advent of building by-laws under the various Public Health Acts was the basis for establishing an adequate standard of domestic building. The basic elements of the structure of a house are its foundations, external walls, floors, and roof. Then there are the secondary elements: windows, doors, partition walls, ceilings; finally the services: water, drainage, electricity, gas.

In order to preserve a basically non-technical approach the method adopted in this handbook has been to treat each of these elements and services in turn, first describing its construction or installation and function, then discussing defects and remedies and normal maintenance which may be necessary. This method has been followed as far as practicable and technical terms are not used unless they are essential. Drawings augment written descriptions or, as far as possible, replace them. It is hoped that this method will facilitate an understanding of all the parts of a house. But it is equally important to have a general picture, so that one has a clear idea of where and when maintenance is critical, where it is not important and where faults are most likely to occur.

House Construction

There are buildings in this country, centuries old, which still provide comfortable homes. Many of these old houses are constructed with frames of English oak and the spaces between the timbers are filled with brick or plaster. They are sometimes described as 'half-timbered' because the oak frame occasionally shows on the out-side of the walls. Oddly enough, although timber-framed houses are a modern form of construction popular in Canada and the United States of America, where the winter is much more severe, and in Australia, they are not often to be found in this country.

The most usual form of construction for private houses in Britain – so usual that it is often termed 'traditional' – is brick load-bearing walls and a timber-framed pitched roof covered with slates or tiles. New forms of construction are generally found only in the larger scale housing, such as are built by local authorities and a few speculative builders. Tall blocks of flats are constructed with steel or concrete frames and the walls are not load-bearing. External walls sometimes take the form of 'cladding', that is slabs of precast concrete or panels of brickwork which are attached to the frame and generally cover it. With a few exceptions most housing of this sort is built by local authorities, many of whom, notably the London County Council, can justly claim not only to have pioneered new techniques of building but also to have contributed some of the best architecture in post-war Britain.

This book is concerned mainly with 'traditional' construction. But whether a house is very old or brand new the basic principles behind the construction are the same and the following chapters should still provide a useful guide.

*

The value of keeping a house in good repair is obvious enough. It can be justified on a number of counts: by ensuring that a house is kept in good condition and by carrying out improvements from time to time its market value will not just be maintained but very likely increased; unexpected catastrophes will, as far as possible, be obviated; the risk of accidents in the home will be reduced; comfortable living conditions will be ensured.

A house, like a motor-car, needs regular maintenance if it is to remain in good condition and continue to perform its function satisfactorily. Naturally not all parts need to be maintained: the foundations, for example, if properly constructed will, under normal circumstances, carry out their function of supporting the house until the day it comes under the demolisher's hammer. Other parts of a house need maintenance only in the sense that they must be inspected periodically to make certain that they are not deteriorating or that anything is going wrong. It is important that defects be remedied before serious deterioration sets in.

The most common cause of damage to a house is water in some form or another: rain, snow, rising damp, even the moisture contained in some building materials, notably concrete and plaster, when a house is new. The effect is not just to ruin the decorations; it can lead to 'blowing' of plaster, decay of brick or stone, the

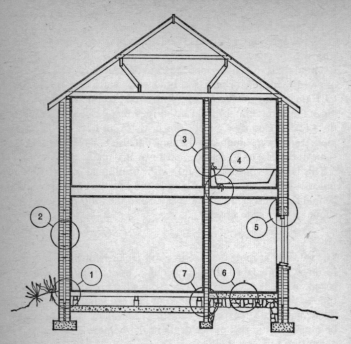

Fig. 1. Common causes of damp and water penetration:
1 Garden soil banked up above dampcourse level
2 Mortar dropping on wall tie, causing cavity bridging
3 Water gets into wall behind bath apron
4 Leaking bath waste connexion
5 Defective flashing at window head
6 No damp-proof membrane on concrete ground floor
7 No damp-proofing to prevent penetration of water through concrete slab into timber floor

rotting of wood. It is ultimately a hazard to the health of the occupants (see fig. 1).

For these reasons it is important to inspect the roof of a house at regular intervals, say once a year, looking in particular for broken or missing slates or tiles, or for fractures in the roof covering if it is a flat roof, for defective flashings, for loose chimney pots and parapet copings, for gutters which have come adrift or are blocked with leaves and rubbish.

The roof space itself should be inspected at least once a year and the roof timbers examined. They may have been attacked by woodworm from an old, infested piece of furniture which has been stored up there. In unventilated places dry rot may have set in as the result of water penetration. This sometimes happens to ground floor timbers. When looking in the roof space the water supply pipes should be examined. If they have been properly lagged against frost it is unlikely there will be any trouble. Inspect the ball valve in the water storage cistern. If water is continuously trickling out and causing the cistern to overflow a new washer is probably needed. Other causes are discussed in chapter 7.

It is important to walk round the house periodically to see that ventilator grilles (air bricks) below ground floor level are not blocked, or that garden soil has not been banked above the level of the dampcourse.

Should the walls of a house be moist it may be the result of rising damp because there is no dampcourse or that it has become defective or, in the case of external walls, because of rain penetration. Remedies are discussed in chapter 3. No doubt regular inspection is not necessary to discover these faults: they would be apparent immediately or have been evident to the surveyor when the house was bought. The important thing is to do something about them; not just patch up and re-decorate, but trace the cause and rectify it.

No paint or varnish or other form of applied decoration lasts indefinitely. Inside the house this may be only a matter of appearance and the frequency of re-decoration depends on a number of factors, including the use to which a room is put (young children's bedrooms, for example, generally suffer severe wear and tear). Externally the condition of surface finishes is much more important. Gutters and downpipes can rust away from their fixings for want of a coat of paint, woodwork can rot (sills of windows and the feet of external door frames are particularly vulnerable). It is unwise to allow the condition of external paintwork to deteriorate. Putting off re-painting for another year will save money for the time being but it could lead to added expenditure later in replacing downpipes which have rusted through or window sills which have rotted.

At some time or another most householders must have experienced some sort of catastrophe in the house, a burst pipe, perhaps, or an overflowing cistern. Many of these need never occur. Burst pipes, for instance, can generally be avoided by lagging them. Some catastrophes, of course, are unavoidable, even when a house is well looked after. Thus it is advisable for every member of the household to know where the main stopcock is located (see chapter 7) and how to turn it off. The stopcock should be checked at least once a year (just before the onset of winter is a good time) to see that it has not become stiff and inoperable. Again it is a sensible precaution to keep spare fusewire of the appropriate rating (see chapter 12) and a small torch near the fuseboard.

Accidents in and around the house are all too frequent. A surprising number of these are caused by something which is in need of repair. It is advisable to make a regular check of those items which, if defective, can be dangerous. These include loose floorboards (especially at the head of stairs), loose or worn stair coverings, loose or missing stair banisters, loose stair handrail, cracked window glass, broken sash cords, defective sash fasteners and window catches, plugs and wiring of electric appliances.

The winter of 1962–3 should have convinced everybody how uncomfortable our houses can be if they are not adequately heated and protected from draughts, and if precautions are not taken against freezing of the water supply. The provision of a heating system itself will not ensure comfortable conditions: heat can escape through the roof if there is no thermal insulation above the top floor ceiling. Adequate thermal insulation and draught-stripping (described in chapter 10) are as important as adequate heating in this climate. Just before winter sets in each year the condition of the heating system or appliances, thermal insulation, draughtstripping, pipe lagging, should all be checked.

Precautions against the winter, however, are not the only matters to be considered in making a house comfortable to live in. There are many items which, though they do not necessarily need regular checking and maintenance, will require attention from time to time. They should not be neglected. They include locks and hinges which need oiling, drawers, doors, and casement sashes which need easing, taps which drip and need new washers, traps under sinks which become blocked or partially blocked and need clearing.

Tools and Materials

It is difficult, if not impossible, to recommend a list of tools for the enthusiastic amateur bent on carrying out his own house maintenance and repairs. But the number and variety of tools which a householder should possess must necessarily depend on the extent of his interest in doing jobs around the house. Comparatively few enthusiasts probably would expect to do all the tasks described in this book. Most people will be more interested in one type of job than another. One householder may be particularly interested in jobs which involve working with wood – making cupboards, easing doors, replacing floorboards – and carpentry tools will obviously form the bulk of his kit. Another may prefer working in metal – repairing gutters, fixing downpipes, mending the plumbing – in which case he will acquire a predominance of plumber's and metalworker's tools. For these reasons it is not proposed to include a comprehensive list of tools. One thing is quite certain. It is not worth having a wide range of tools if you do not know how to use them properly; if, in other words, you have not a natural aptitude or have not received instruction. For a surprising number of jobs around the house a few basic tools will do. These comprise a small screwdriver for electrical work (replacing fusewire, wiring plugs, etc.), a larger screwdriver (say a 4-in. long blade), a bradawl, a claw hammer, a pair of pliers, and a wrench.

Obviously for more ambitious work, including some of the jobs described in this book, this minimum list will not be sufficient. But the acquiring of additional tools is a matter of commonsense in which one or two principles should be followed. Cheap tools are seldom worth the money, even for the clumsiest amateur. It is better to start with a modest set of basic tools and add to it as skill and interest develop. Most manufacturers of good quality tools have catalogues which are worth looking through before tools are purchased. If you are fortunate enough to know a carpenter, a plumber, or a bricklayer do not hesitate to seek his advice about tools. Otherwise ask the local supplier.

Over the last few years a large number of power tools has come on to the domestic market. It goes without saying that extra care is needed in their use. They are a great help to the home handyman but are potentially dangerous if handled casually. The Consumers' Association carried out tests on a number of makes and the results were published in *Which* (November 1959 and December 1963), the Association's journal. The tests revealed that not all models were electrically safe. Recommendations were made for best buys.

Tools and equipment for house decoration present a problem. This is because decorating is work which requires considerable paraphernalia yet it is not normally done often. Many householders may not be aware that it is possible to hire decorators' tools and equipment – anything from a paint roller to a set of trestles and a board for paperhanging. It is also possible to hire power tools such as sanders, polishers, and paint sprays. Names of firms can be found in the classified telephone directory.

The materials required for house maintenance and repairs are obtainable from ironmongers and builders' merchants. In addition most chain stores and many department stores have a home handyman or do-it-yourself section selling tools, nails, screws, paint, electrical accessories, etc. Ironmongers sell hinges, locks, door handles and catches, nails, screws, washers, and generally all sorts of hand and small power tools. There is invariably an ironmonger in every High Street. It is worth getting to know the proprietor. He is often an enthusiast himself and usually has a considerable knowledge of tools and their uses and the bits and pieces needed for everyday house repairs and maintenance. Building materials such as wallboards, guttering, cement, putty, glass, paint, wallpaper, etc. are generally only found at a builders' merchant. Timber is best obtained from a timber merchant rather than a do-it-yourself shop. There is a wider range of lengths and sections and generally a better quality of timber available. Most districts have a timber yard which stocks plywood, blockboard, and wallboards as well as sawn and planed timber. Even a small yard has fairly extensive stocks of softwood of the sizes needed for house maintenance and repairs. Hardwood, however, is not so common and if you want a particular species or a particular section you will almost certainly have to go farther afield to a yard specializing in this wood.

House maintenance is not something to be shrugged off, nor should you be put off by the amount of checking there is to do. Detection and prevention in all cases are better than cure, and if these are done in time the cure itself will not, in most cases, be beyond the capable amateur, for whom this book has been written.

CHAPTER 2

Roofs

The roof is the most exposed part of a house and hence the most vulnerable to the elements. The moment a leak appears, no matter how small, its cause should be traced and the damage repaired. This chapter deals with roof construction and the various forms of roof coverings used both on pitched and flat roofs. It describes defects which sometimes occur and gives details for remedying them when the methods are within the scope of the amateur. Finally there are two check lists. The first covers possible causes of roof leaks and is intended to guide the householder in diagnosing the cause of trouble. The second list is to be used when periodic maintenance inspection is carried out. If the inspection is to be done by a builder or a plumber he should be asked to check these points in particular.

Pitched roofs

The principal elements in a timber-framed pitched roof are the rafters (fig. 2). They form the slope of the roof and carry the roof covering, and are usually spaced about 16 ins. apart. Tiles, slates, and shingles must have closely spaced supports and are normally fixed to battens which are pieces of timber, small in cross section (usually about $1\frac{1}{2}$ ins. wide $\times$ 1 in. thick), nailed to the rafters at right angles to them. At one time it was common practice to cover the whole of the roof with timber boarding before laying tiles or slates. Boarding serves three useful functions: (i) it helps strengthen or 'stiffen' the roof; (ii) it provides a second line of defence against rain or snow penetration, and (iii) it makes a warmer house. This last function is discussed in the chapter on insulation. The high cost of timber and the fact that its use as roof boarding was not permitted for a period during and after the war has almost brought this practice to an end.

Tiles and slates are usually laid over a waterproof roofing felt.

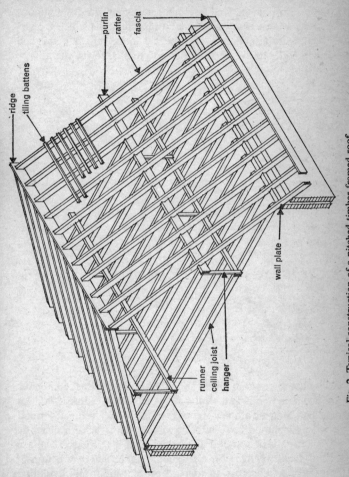

Fig. 2. Typical construction of a pitched timber-framed roof

This prevents snow and driving rain from penetrating between the joints of the tiles or slates, something which can happen even in a well constructed roof. Roofing felt is sold by builders' merchants in rolls 32 ins. wide. The development of reinforced bituminous felts on a woven base has resulted in roofing felts which are virtually untearable and may safely be laid across rafters. Felt is laid at right angles to the slope of the roof, that is, across the rafters.

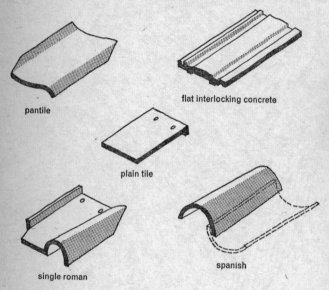

Fig. 3. Types of roofing tile

Each successive width of roll should be lapped at least 6 ins. over the previous one if laid straight on the rafters, 3 ins. if laid on boarding, starting at the lower edge of the roof. The lap at the end of a length should be 6 ins. The roofing felt is held in place by nailing battens on top of it along the line of the rafters. These are termed *counter battens*. Shingles should not be laid over boarding or roofing felt because this would prevent air from circulating underneath the shingles and could cause rot.

The form of roof, i.e. pitched or flat, largely dictates the type of roof covering used. A pitched roof, because of its slope, sheds water quickly. Thus the covering can take the form of small units: tiles, slates, or shingles where the units overlap and the joints are not sealed. Most materials used as flat roof coverings, e.g. asphalt, sheet copper, or lead, are suitable for pitched roofs, but are less commonly used than small unit coverings.

Tiles. Roofing tiles are made out of clay or concrete. They are manufactured in a variety of patterns (fig. 3). The simplest, called a *plain* tile, has projections or nibs formed on the underside at the top edge. These hook over the battens when the tiles are laid, holding them in position. In addition every fourth or fifth course of tiles is nailed to the battens through holes formed in the tiles

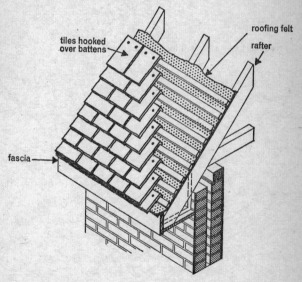

Fig. 4. Laying plain tiles

during manufacture (fig. 4). These tiles rely on a double overlap for watertightness. More complicated patterns incorporate inter-locking edges and generally are laid only with a single lap.

Slates. Unlike plain tiles, slates do not have nibs and every slate, therefore, must be nailed to the battens. If a single slate works

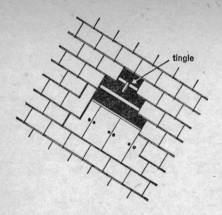

1 Remove defective slates, nail lead tingle to batten

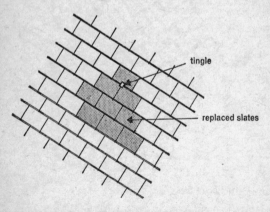

2 Replace slates by nailing, secure final slate with tingle

Fig. 5. Replacing slates with the use of a tingle

loose, however, it is not possible to nail it back in position. It must be secured in place by a *tingle*, which is a strip of lead nailed to the batten or boarding before the slate is placed back (fig. 5). When the slate is positioned the tingle is bent over its end to stop it slipping down out of position again. If it is necessary to replace a number of slates it can still be done with only one tingle. Slates are replaced one at a time starting on the lowest row of the area to be replaced. It will be found that each slate in turn, with the exception of the very last (highest) slate, can be nailed as it is positioned. Those on either edge of the exposed area have to be pushed half under the adjoining slates which have not been removed and can thus only be fixed with one nail. In the centre of the exposed area each slate can be fixed with two nails. Finally the last slate is secured with a tingle as described above.

Shingles. Oak shingles are a traditional roof covering dating back to the Romans and Saxons. Nowadays western red cedar shingles are more common. They are usually made 16 ins. long and are nailed to battens spaced 5 ins. from centre to centre.

Asbestos cement. Asbestos cement, composed of asbestos fibres and Portland cement, is available in the form of slates or corrugated sheets. Slates are laid in much the same way as ordinary slates.

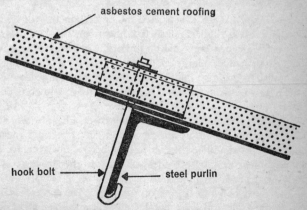

asbestos cement roofing

hook bolt ———   — steel purlin

Fig. 6. Hook bolt securing asbestos cement roofing

A timber-framed pitched roof covered with corrugated asbestos cement sheets is not normally constructed in exactly the same way as one covered with slates or tiles. Instead of rafters, purlins are used, laid at right angles to the slope of the roof. Purlins are usually spaced more widely apart than rafters and are supported on trusses. The usual method of securing corrugated asbestos cement sheets in position is to drill holes in the sheets and either nail direct into the purlin, if it is timber, or use *hook bolts* (fig. 6) if it is a steel purlin.

Sheet metal. Aluminium, copper, lead, and zinc in large sheets are sometimes used as pitched roof coverings, but are more commonly used on flat roofs (see p. 27). Aluminium is also manufactured in corrugated sheet form and is fixed in a similar way to asbestos cement. Fixing methods are similar to those for flat roofs. On aluminium and copper sheet covered roofs with pitches over 15°, *standing seam* joints are generally used instead of wood rolls. Because of its weight, lead sheet has a tendency to slip or creep and, on pitched roofs, must be securely fixed to the decking. This is normally done by nailing the top edges of the sheets with large flat-headed copper nails.

Flat roofs

Most flat roofs are constructed either of concrete or timber. Timber roofs are built similarly to timber floors (fig. 7). Joists span between walls or beams and on top of these a decking is laid (as on a ship). Timber boards are the traditional form of decking and are nailed to the joists. Nowadays other materials are also used as decking: woodwool, in slabs 2 ins. or 3 ins. thick, strawboard, and fibreboard.

The main function of decking is to provide a base on which the roof covering is laid, as almost all flat roof coverings must be fully supported, unlike tiles which span between battens. In addition a timber decking provides stiffening to the structure of the roof, just as boarding does on a pitched roof.

The most common forms of flat roof covering are asphalt, bituminous felt, and sheet metal. Generally speaking, sheet metal roofs, fixed by traditional methods, employ *mechanical* joints: single or double lock cross welts, standing seams, wood-filled or

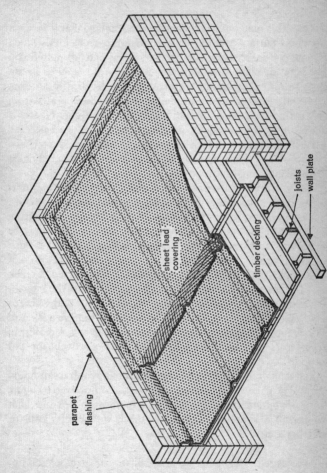

Fig. 7. Typical construction of a flat timber-framed roof

hollow rolls. Asphalt, by its nature, is jointless, and bituminous felt has its joints sealed with bitumen, the material with which it is stuck down.

Asphalt. This material has the inherent advantage that it forms a continuous surface over the whole roof, unbroken by joints which are potential sources of leaks. Parapet, valley, and box gutters can also be formed in asphalt as well as flashings. It is applied in hot liquid form, poured on to the decking, and levelled to an even depth with a trowel. A good asphalt roof should be separated from the decking by a layer of roofing felt. This prevents blistering caused by pockets of air or moisture trapped between decking and asphalt. It also isolates the asphalt from movement in the structure. The laying of an asphalt roof is the job of a specialist roofing contractor (see appendix 1).

Surface crazing is not uncommon, and is no cause for alarm. It results from sunshine causing hardening and slight shrinkage. Cracks, however, are more serious. They generally result from movement of the supporting structure or decking. This may be particularly so where the supporting structure is concrete. Such cracks, however, can even be caused by the shrinkage of a coat of paint applied at some time to the asphalt. Once started, a crack tends to deepen until it is right through the thickness of the asphalt. Where the roof is paved for walking on, movement of the tiles or paving slabs can cause cracking. It is advisable to have a layer of sand, gravel, or building paper between asphalt and decking; in recent years polythene sheet has been used effectively for this purpose.

If an asphalt roof is in need of repair a roofing contractor should be called in. Cracks can be temporarily repaired, however, by filling them with bitumen paint, obtainable at hardware shops and paint suppliers. The simplest way to apply this is with a putty knife or stripping knife.

Bituminous felt. This material, like asphalt, can also be used not only as a roof covering but also for gutters and flashings. Although suitable for flat roofs, it should always have a slight fall, say 2 ins. in 10 ft. Felts are of three kinds: organic fibre, asbestos-based or glass fibre. The material is laid in hot liquid bitumen. A roof consists of two or three separate layers bonded together by the hot bitumen: it is for this reason that this form of roof covering is often called built-up roofing. The surface of the top layer is normally coated with either mineral granules, applied to the felt at the factory, or stone chippings bedded in hot bitumen on the site. The laying of bitumen felt, as described above, is the job of a roofing contractor (see appendix 1). It is possible, however, to purchase rolls of felt from builders' merchants and lay it yourself by nailing it to the roof boarding. This is satisfactory for outbuildings – fuel bunkers, garden sheds, and garages – but is not suitable for more permanent situations such as the roof of the house itself.

The most common defect is blistering of the felt. This occurs when the sun heats the roof, causing moisture, which is trapped within the supporting structure or decking or between layers of

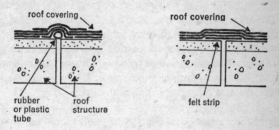

Fig. 8. Movement joints in built-up roofing

felt, to vaporize. The moisture vapour expands, causing a build-up of pressure under the felt and hence the blisters.

Splitting of the felt may occur as the result of movement in the supporting structure. Even where joints have been formed in the structure to take up movement due to expansion or contraction, such splitting is inevitable if the felt covering itself does not also have a joint at these points. Two ways of forming this joint are shown in fig. 8.

Major repairs should be left to a roofing contractor. Temporary or minor repairs can be done with bitumen paint applied with a putty knife or stripping knife.

Sheet metal. Aluminium, copper, lead, and zinc in large flat sheets (that is, not corrugated) are commonly used as coverings on flat roofs. On exposure to the atmosphere the metals oxidize, forming a film or patina which acts as a protective coating. Sheet metal roofs should be laid by a competent plumber with experience in this sort of work. It is not a job for the amateur. Joints between sheets running down the slope of the roof are usually formed with wood rolls. An underlay of roofing felt should be fixed to the boarding before the sheet metal covering is laid.

Repeated walking on sheet metal roof coverings is the most frequent cause of damage. But damage can be precipitated by defects in the decking, such as the warping of timber boards.

Aluminium, lead, and zinc are likely to be affected by mortar and, where they are in contact with or embedded in mortar, should be coated liberally with bitumen paint. Lead is sensitive to attack by acids such as are present in oak and unseasoned softwoods.

The repair of sheet metal roofs is a skilled job and should be left to the plumber. Most plumbers are familiar with the techniques of laying sheet lead roofing and many with copper and zinc.

Emergency repairs can be carried out with bitumen paint, coated liberally over a break or fracture. This should, however, be regarded only as a temporary expedient. It may make the subsequent permanent repair more difficult.

Traffic on flat roof surfaces. Sheet metal roofs should not be walked on. If occasional foot traffic is expected, it is usual nowadays for the architect to specify a heavier gauge of metal. In older houses it is unlikely that such provision will have been made. If you can get on to your flat roof fairly easily and want to make use of it as a roof terrace, it will be necessary to lay timber duckboards on the roof surface between the wood rolls.

Duckboards can be constructed with 3-in. × 1½-in. bearers and 3-in. × 1-in. battens nailed to them and spaced 1 in. apart. Use 2-in. nails for fixing, two to each bearer. The width of the duckboard will be governed by the spacing of the rolls on the roof. The length should be limited for easy handling of each section, say 4 ft. It will be necessary to take them up from time to time to clear leaves and rubbish which may have accumulated underneath. If you use softwood, creosote all surfaces of the timber. Otherwise use a hardwood such as elm.

If the roof is of bituminous felt or asphalt, it is worth considering tiles laid on top of the roof covering to provide a terrace surface. Asbestos cement and precast concrete tiles are available for this purpose. They are usually bedded to the roof surface in hot bitumen. The Building Centre will provide details of manufacturers and suppliers.

Gutters and downpipes

Cast-iron gutters should be inspected regularly for damage caused by rusting of the bolts and deterioration of the putty at joints. Mastic compounds are available from builders merchants for repairing defective joints, and it is a wise precaution to paint the inside of metal gutters with bituminous paint. Do not forget to

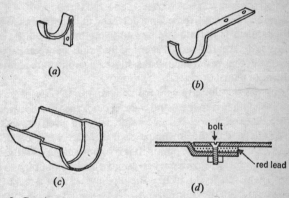

Fig. 9. Cast-iron gutter components and details (*a*) bracket for fixing to fascia or rafter feet; (*b*) bracket for fixing to top of rafter; (*c*) socket end of gutter; (*d*) fixing lengths of gutter together

repaint as the need arises. Apart from blockages caused by leaves, gutters often overflow because lengths between downpipes sag through failure at the joints. Make sure that the brackets supporting the gutter have not come adrift from the fascia board or rafter feet (see fig. 9).

All gutters should have continuous falls to the downpipes, otherwise they are likely to overflow. It is surprising how often this is overlooked.

If a length of gutter is allowed to deteriorate so that there are several holes or breaks in it, replacement is necessary. However, individual holes can be repaired by one of a number of techniques. For the amateur one of the simplest is with the use of a form of epoxy resin compound available from builders' merchants or do-it-yourself shops. The area around the hole should be brushed clean of flaking rust and other débris by means of a wire brush. The compound should be mixed and spread on to a piece of paper large enough to cover the hole. This should then be pressed over the hole so that compound squeezes through it. The compound on the inside of the gutter should then be smoothed off. After allowing time to dry and set, the paper can be rubbed off and the hole is thus repaired. The same technique can be used in repairing downpipes except that it is not possible to get at the inside of the downpipe to smooth off the compound which has squeezed through.

Downpipes are likely to become detached at their fixings. What usually happens is that downpipe and fixing bracket come away from the wall. Apart from weakening the joints between lengths of downpipe, thus resulting in leaks, loose downpipes are a potential source of danger.

Downpipes should have wire balloons on top to prevent leaves and rubbish falling into them and causing blockages. If a downpipe becomes blocked it will become evident by an overflow in the gutter at the head of the downpipe or, if there are weak joints, by water spurting out at these points. If it is impossible to dislodge an obstruction, it may be necessary to remove a section of pipe to do so. But it is worth trying to free the pipe by pushing a length of stout wire up from the bottom.

Flashings

Where a roof abuts a party wall or where a chimney stack passes through the roof, for example, it is necessary to make a watertight joint between roof surface and brickwork. This is done with a *flashing* and with a pitched roof it is known as *step flashing* (fig. 10).

It is necessary to have a flashing around all projections through the roof: pipes, rooflights, dormer windows, etc. Flashings are usually metal, either lead, zinc, or copper. They are a potential source of roof leaks; they may become dislodged by high winds or they may develop holes. Defective flashings should be repaired or replaced immediately, even if there is no apparent leak. Water entering at these points may do so slowly but damp areas inside the house will eventually be evident. Chimney breasts often show the first signs of damp due to this cause. The repair of metal flashings is a job for a plumber who has the right tools. Working the metal into the required shapes for flashing is a skilled job. It is often necessary temporarily to remove and then replace some of the roof

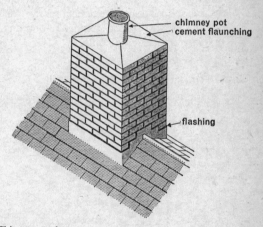

Fig. 10. Chimney stack

covering in order to get the new flashing under it and, where flashing is built into brickwork, lead wedges must be inserted.

Flashings sometimes are formed in cement mortar. They are not as good as metal flashings; they do not give with roof movement and consequently tend to crack. This is particularly likely at the junction with brickwork or roof covering. Cement mortar flashings (or cement *fillets* as they are sometimes called) need to be inspected more frequently than metal. Cracks should be repaired immediately. The simplest way is to purchase a bag of ready-mixed cement mortar from a builders' merchant or hardware store. This needs only to be mixed with water to be ready for use.

Make sure you brush out and clear away all loose and broken pieces and all crumbled mortar before putting any new mortar in position. It may be necessary to chip off cracked pieces with a cold chisel.

Chimneys

If there are chimney pots on your chimney stack, make sure they are not cracked or loose. A falling pot may damage the roof and could also cause serious accidents. Check the cement *flaunching* on top of the chimney stack. If it is cracked or broken, repair it with cement mortar as described above for cement mortar flashings.

The joints of the brickwork may require re-pointing. This is discussed in the chapter on external walls.

Parapets

Parapets are external walls of a building which have been carried

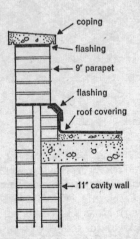

coping
flashing
9″ parapet
flashing
roof covering
11″ cavity wall

Fig. 11. Parapet construction

up above roof level (fig. 11). They are finished on top with a coping: brick on edge, concrete, or stone. The purpose of the coping is to protect the top of the brick wall from rain penetration.

Copings should be inspected regularly as, like chimney pots, they can become loose and fall off. If this occurs, the old bedding mortar must be hacked out, and the coping rebedded in fresh mortar.

Rooflights

Because of its position the glass in a rooflight is more vulnerable than that in a window. Cracked glass should be replaced as soon as possible. If you are applying draught stripping to windows, do not forget the rooflights. They are a particularly bad source of draughts.

Roof leaks: check list

When rain or snow causes a leak it is usually the result of:

(*a*) A dislodged or cracked tile or slate. Regular inspection of the roof may forestall this, but there is always the possibility of a high wind blowing a tile or slate off the roof. The replacing of a single tile is generally simpler than replacing a slate, since tiles are either interlocking or, in the case of plain tiles, have a nib which hooks over the batten. Thus it is not necessary to nail individual tiles in position: it is usually sufficient to force it over the batten and into position between adjoining tiles.

(*b*) Rain or fine powdery snow being blown up under the joints of the tiles or slates. This will cause no trouble if a good quality roofing felt has been laid under the roof covering.

(*c*) Gutters becoming choked with leaves. This will not occur if gutters are inspected and cleared out regularly.

(*d*) Defective flashings (see p. 30). Again, regular inspection of the roof should forestall this.

Maintenance: check list

The roof of a house, gutters, chimneys, parapets, flashings, etc., should be inspected regularly, say once a year. If the roof is reasonably accessible from a ladder or through a roof hatch from within the house and if you have a good head for heights, there is no reason why you should not carry out an inspection yourself. Otherwise call in a builder or plumber. In particular check the following:

1 Tiles or slates which have cracked or become dislodged. Valley and hip tiles are particularly vulnerable.

2 Surface cracking or excessive blistering of bituminous felt or asphalt roof surfaces.

3 Gutters choked with leaves. When examining gutters make sure the joints between lengths are sound and that the gutters are securely attached to their supporting brackets.

4 Rainwater outlets, hopper heads choked with leaves. Make sure that all outlets and indeed all pipes through the roof have wire balloons on top and that these are secure. Check that all down-pipes are securely fixed to their supports. Make at least one inspection of gutters and downpipes during heavy rain as blockages and overflows will then be very obvious. If the outlet from a gutter or any part of the downpipe itself has become blocked, you will see water spurting out of the joints of the downpipe.

5 Loose copings on parapet walls.

6 Loose or cracked chimney pots. Defective flaunching.

7 Defective pointing of the chimney stack.

8 Defective flashings. Do not forget to examine flashings around rooflights and around pipes projecting through the roof.

CHAPTER 3

External walls

The major function of the external walls of a house is to support the upper floors and roof. Not all houses have load-bearing walls, however. Maisonettes and multi-storey flats, for example, are usually constructed so that floors and roof are supported on a structural frame of steel or reinforced concrete. The external walls of the average bungalow or semi-detached house, on the other hand, are generally load-bearing. It is interesting to note that, in such cases, the thickness of the wall in brick or stone houses is determined not so much on the requirements of strength as on the need for effective protection from the weather.

Brick walls

Cavity construction. In modern brick houses external walls are generally built in cavity construction, comprising two single thicknesses of brick separated by a 2-in. wide cavity or air space (fig. 12). The cavity prevents penetration by rain and also provides a measure of thermal insulation. A cavity wall permits less heat to escape from the house than does a 9-in. thick solid wall, and uses fewer facing bricks per square yard, though both use the same total number of bricks. The thermal insulation standard of a cavity wall can be further improved by using lightweight concrete blocks for the inner leaf of the wall. Such construction is common practice these days as it is cheaper and reduces the dead weight of the wall. In cavity construction the two leaves of the wall are tied together by means of galvanized metal wall ties (fig. 13).

Solid construction. Older houses are more likely to have solid walls. The walls are thick because it is their thickness which keeps out the weather. Rain which penetrates the outer surface of the wall dries out before reaching the inner surface. 9-in. solid walls are not usually thick enough to stop rain penetration causing damp patches

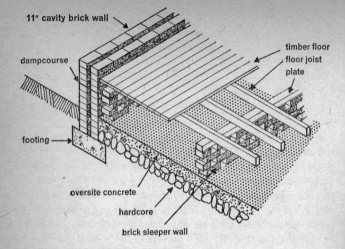

Fig. 12. Cavity wall construction, timber ground floor

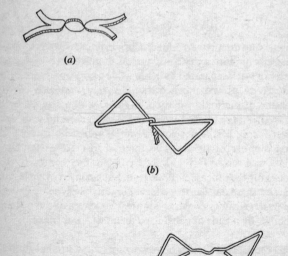

Fig. 13. Wall ties (*a*) vertical twist; (*b*) butterfly; (*c*) double triangle

inside the house, but are satisfactory if covered on the outside with stucco or cement-lime-sand rendering.

Stone walls

External walls of natural stone are a traditional construction in many parts of the country, two examples being flint walls, common in the chalk districts, and Kentish rag. In house building, stone walls can generally be classified as either rubble or ashlar. Rubble walls are those built of thinly bedded stones of irregular shapes as in random rubble or squared as in coursed rubble. Examples are shown in fig. 14. Ashlar is the term given to stones which are dressed with a special tool, a scabbling hammer, or sawn to blocks of given dimensions. Because of the expense of dressing ashlar it is usually employed as a facing to the wall with a rubble or brick backing.

Concrete walls

Ordinary reinforced concrete is a very popular material in industrial and commercial building, where it is normally employed as the frame in framed construction, but it is not commonly used in housing. *No-fines* concrete is a type in which the mix does not contain sand and, provided the external surface is rendered, it makes a very satisfactory wall. Considerable development has recently taken place in the use of lightweight aggregate for concrete and this material has good thermal insulation properties.

Timber walls

Although timber framed walls are commonly used in house building in North America, Australia, and elsewhere they are still comparatively rare in this country. Timber framing comprises uprights, termed *studs*, spaced 16 ins. to 18 ins. apart, horizontal top and bottom members, called *plates*, into which the studs are housed and nailed, and short horizontal members, known as *nogging*, which are fitted between the studs to give rigidity (fig. 15). Diagonal bracing is let into the face of the studs.

Timber framing may be covered externally with such materials as timber weatherboards or vertical boarding, tiles or asbestos

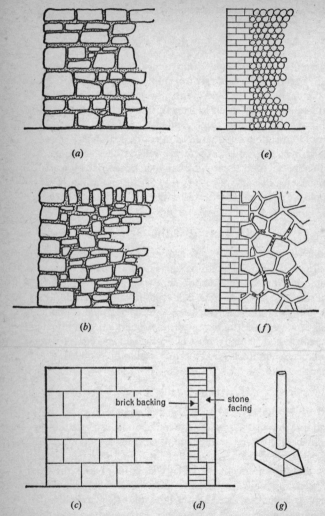

Fig. 14. Types of stone wall (*a*) coursed rubble; (*b*) random rubble;
(*c*) ashlar; (*d*) section through an ashlar wall; (*e*) flint; (*f*) Kentish rag;
(*g*) scabbling hammer

cement sheets. Internally, plasterboard, timber boarding, fibre-board, or other wall board linings may be used. Thermal insulation is an important element in this form of construction and it is also

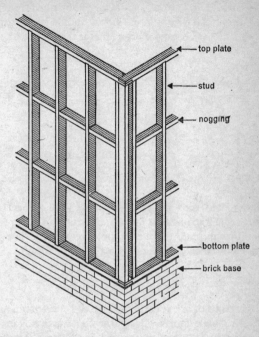

Fig. 15. Timber framed wall construction

desirable to tack waterproof building paper, laid horizontally, to the framing behind the external lining.

Fixing to walls

Methods of making a fixing into a masonry wall for the purpose of hanging a picture or fitting shelves are described in chapter 6.

Pointing

Brick and stone walls often have their joints *pointed*. This is a technique in which mortar is trowelled into the joint after the wall is built (fig. 16). In existing walls it is quite usual to point the joints when the old mortar has come away along the edges. To point (or re-point) a wall the procedure is first to rake out the joints to a depth of about ¾ in. The wall should then be brushed to remove dust and loose material. The pointing mortar should be not appreciably stronger than the bedding mortar, that is the mortar in which the

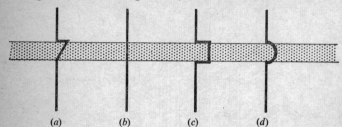

Fig. 16. Finishes to brickwork joints (*a*) struck; (*b*) flush; (*c*) recessed; (*d*) keyed

bricks were laid. As a guide, it should not be a stronger mix than one part cement to one part lime to six parts sand. Before applying the pointing mortar, the wall should be wetted. The pointing mortar should then be applied with a pointing trowel.

Defects and remedies

Defects in walls of brick, natural stone, or concrete can usually be traced to a single fault in design or construction. Less often a combination of faults contributes to a single defect. It is not always easy for the expert, let alone the householder, to discover the cause of a particular fault. To assist diagnosis a number of commonly encountered defects are described on the following pages. Recommended remedies are also given.

Rain penetration of solid walls

In a solid wall (i.e. one without a cavity) damp may appear on the internal surface as the result of penetration by driving rain, particularly if the wall is in an exposed position. There are several treatments for overcoming this, some of which are described below. Those which can with care be applied by the householder himself are so indicated. The remainder are only suitable for application by skilled workers and a builder should be called in. Treatments may be applied either to the external or the internal surface of the wall. Generally, external treatments have the advantage that they keep the wall dry, hence improving durability and, at the same time, keeping the house warmer.

External treatments

Tile or slate hanging. One of the most effective treatments of a masonry wall through which rain is penetrating is to hang tiles or slates on the external surface of the wall. This is a traditional way

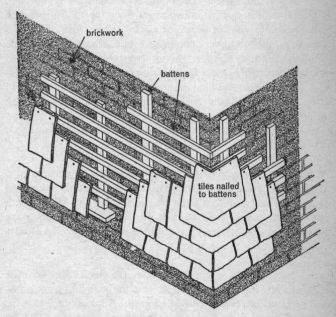

Fig. 17. Tile hanging on a masonry wall

of finishing external walls in many parts of the country. The tiles or slates can be applied to a masonry wall or to timber framing (fig. 17). The procedure is to attach vertical battens to the external wall face by means of masonry plugs and screws, nail horizontal battens to these, and fix the tiles or slates to the horizontal battens. Each tile or slate must, of course, be nailed to the battens. The durability of the treatment is improved if battens are pressure-impregnated with preservative beforehand. It is possible to buy timber which has had this treatment. Names of yards which stock this timber are available from the Timber Research and Development Association (see appendix 2).

Render. Rain penetration may be prevented by rendering the whole of the external face of the wall. It is first necessary to rake out the joints to a depth of about $\frac{1}{2}$ in. and clean off all loose material with a stiff wire brush. The surface should be wetted before rendering. Render should be applied in two coats, using the same mix for the undercoat as for the finishing coat, each $\frac{3}{8}$ to $\frac{1}{2}$ in. thick. If the wall is exposed, the mix should comprise 1 part cement to 1 part lime to 6 parts sand, by volume. The undercoat should be allowed to dry out thoroughly before the finishing coat is applied. If practicable, allow at least two days in summer and a week or more in cold or wet weather. The surface should be dampened before applying the finishing coat. If the wall is reasonably sheltered, a mix of 1 part cement to 2 parts lime to 9 parts sand is adequate. A wood float should be used rather than a steel trowel.

Pebble dash is an alternative to smooth render. It consists of a rough finish of small pebbles or crushed stone, graded from about $\frac{1}{4}$ to $\frac{1}{2}$ in., thrown on to a fresh coat of mortar and left exposed. The undercoat and finishing coat on to which the pebbles are thrown should comprise 1 part cement to $\frac{1}{2}$ part lime to 3 parts sand by volume.

Roughcast is another alternative. It is a finish which is thrown on as a wet mix and left rough. The aggregate in the finishing coat consists of sand and crushed stone or gravel from about $\frac{1}{4}$ to $\frac{1}{2}$ in. Mix should comprise 1 part cement to 3 parts aggregate by volume.

Cement paint. Provided there are no large cracks or defects in the external surface of the wall which would permit water penetration behind the paint film, a cement paint coating can be quite effective.

A description of the preparation of the surface and the application of the paint is given in chapter 14. The treatment can be applied by the amateur.

Oil, bitumen, or tar paint give an almost impervious coating. It is important, therefore, to be quite sure that other causes of damp penetration, such as through parapets or window sills, are not present, because, if they are, treatment of the external face of the wall with these paints will trap the damp in the wall. A description of the preparation of the surface and the application of the paint is given in chapter 14. The treatment can be applied by the amateur.

Colourless waterproofer. If the appearance of the wall is to be retained a colourless waterproofing liquid should be used. Colourless waterproofers take the form of solutions or emulsions of water-repellent substances and in recent years considerable development has taken place in the application of silicones for this purpose. Since they are marketed as proprietary solutions the manufacturer's instructions must be carefully followed. Names and addresses of manufacturers are available from the Building Centre (see appendix 2). It is likely, with this form of treatment, that regular re-treatment will be necessary. The treatment can be applied by the amateur.

Internal treatments

If it is not certain that rain penetration is the sole cause of damp, it is advisable to employ a treatment applied to the internal surface of the wall. One disadvantage of external treatments, with the exception of the hanging of tiles or slates, is that, if they are not porous, any damp in the wall, due to rising damp for example, will not be able to dry out through the external surface. Thus the effect of using a non-porous external treatment may actually aggravate the condition. Internal treatments, on the other hand, will not do so in any way and have the added advantage that they are applied to a more accessible surface.

Dry lining is an effective internal treatment (fig. 18). It involves fixing vertical timber battens to the internal surface of the wall and nailing wall boards to them to form a new internal surface. The treatment means, in effect, isolating the internal wall surface from the damp. It is also an effective means of improving the thermal insulation of the wall, thus reducing or even eliminating condensation. This treatment may be used when rising damp is the cause of the trouble.

Battens should be pressure-impregnated with preservative. To

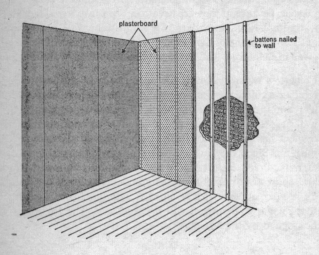

Fig. 18. Dry lining

avoid the risk of staining the plasterboard and decorations, creosote should not be used for this purpose. Battens should be $1\frac{5}{8}$ ins. $\times \frac{5}{8}$ in. and spaced at not more than 18 ins. from centre to centre or to suit the width of a sheet of plasterboard. Plasterboard should be $\frac{3}{8}$ in. thick and foil-backed. It is usually obtainable in 6-ft $\times$ 3-ft and 8-ft $\times$ 4-ft boards; as joints should be reduced to a minimum the larger size sheet should be used wherever possible. For 3-ft wide sheets of plasterboard 18-in. centres are suitable, for 4-ft wide plasterboard 16-in. centres will be necessary. By using chrome-steel nails the battens can be fixed direct into the brickwork provided it is not too soft. As a guide, four $1\frac{1}{2}$-in. $\times \frac{1}{8}$-in. chrome-steel nails are sufficient to fix an 8-ft batten to fletton brickwork. Fix the plasterboard to the battens with 1-in. galvanized steel clouts, taking care not to puncture the surface of the plasterboard around the clout head. Clouts should be spaced approximately 9 ins. apart.

If it is intended to paint direct on to the plasterboard it will be necessary to provide a virtually invisible joint between boards. In this case tapered or recessed edge boards should be used. If wallpaper is to be the finish and providing the paper has slight texture or some pattern an ordinary butt joint between boards will be quite satisfactory.

Rain penetration of cavity walls

Rain penetration may occur, even in a cavity wall. This happens when the cavity has been 'bridged', for example by mortar droppings on a wall tie which thus provide a continuous passage for water (fig. 19). The only effective answer is to remove one or two

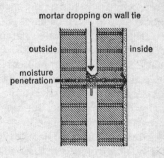

Fig. 19. Cavity bridging

bricks from the outer skin of the wall over the area where damp has occurred, and dislodge the mortar droppings.

Damp patches may occur above the heads of openings in a cavity wall. This, again, is probably due to mortar droppings and even when there is flashing above the opening, damp will penetrate. Again the only effective cure is to take out some bricks and remove the obstruction.

Rain penetration of external rendered surfaces. If the *external* surface of a wall is already rendered, rain may still penetrate if substantial cracks have developed in the render. The cure is not necessarily as simple a matter as repairing the cracks, for if they are substantial there is very likely some other cause at work, such as foundation movement, sulphate attack of the brickwork, or an incorrect mix for the render in the first place. It is advisable in such cases to obtain expert advice from an architect.

Frost

The action of frost may cause (i) powdering of the surface of soft bricks, (ii) flaking of bricks whose frost resistance is too low for the particular exposure conditions, (iii) displacement of strong pointing mortar covering a weak building mortar, (iv) crumbling of the surface of porous mortar joints.

It is important to note that the above defects, if apparent, may not necessarily have been caused by frost. They may be due in the first place to other causes and frost has simply aggravated failure. Generally, brickwork is only likely to be damaged by frost when soaked with water, hence retaining walls, parapets, and free-standing walls are vulnerable. It is rare to see frost attack on brickwork in ordinary external walls to houses. During a frost, water in the wall expands and may break up the bricks or the mortar. New brickwork is particularly susceptible because of the wet state of the brickwork during drying out and because of the low strength of the mortar during this period.

If frost attack is extensive it may be necessary to rebuild the brickwork. If only a small area has been affected, however, it is possible to cut out the damaged brickwork and replace it with sound bricks or brick slips 1 in. thick having a frost resistance high enough to resist the conditions of exposure. It is advisable to seek expert advice on this.

Damp

If the house has no dampcourse, or the dampcourse has become defective, patches of rising damp may appear in ground-floor rooms. The effect of rising damp is a more or less continuous band of discoloration showing on the internal surface of the wall for a height of from 1 ft to 3 ft and sometimes higher.

Even when there is a dampcourse and it is effective, rising damp may occur due to the ground level having been inadvertently raised such as by forming a garden bed against the wall of the house. The cure for this, of course, is to lower the garden bed to a level at least 6 ins. below the dampcourse.

Inserting a dampcourse. It is possible to have a dampcourse inserted into the walls, but the process, whilst effective, is relatively costly. It is usually carried out by specialist firms whose names and addresses can be obtained from Building Centres (see appendix 2).

Cement render. An alternative is to apply a waterproof cement render to the inside face of the affected walls. The existing plaster should be hacked off with a bricklayer's chisel and hammer to a height of at least 2 ft above the level of damp penetration. The render should be applied in two coats to a total thickness of $\frac{3}{4}$ in.

It is important, when this treatment is used, that the outside face of the wall has no rendering. Otherwise the wall will, in effect, become sealed; there is no exposed surface through which moisture can dry out, and the damp will have no alternative but to continue to rise up the wall.

Leaking pipes. Do not overlook the fact that damp patches on a wall may be the result of a leaking pipe. Take care to examine the possibilities of this before assuming some other cause. Damaged or defective rainwater pipes and gutters can very easily lead to damp walls if not attended to promptly. In both cases the joints are points of weakness. The trouble may be simply blockage at the head of the rainwater pipe or of a gutter with leaves and rubbish. This is particularly likely to happen in inaccessible places such as box gutters behind parapet walls.

Leaks in the water service or the waste system may be more difficult to trace. Again the weak points are the joints. Moisture around a pipe, however, is not necessarily a sign that the pipe is leaking. If the air is humid, condensation often forms on the cold water pipes and this moisture may accumulate in positions where it can cause dampness. The coldest pipe in a house is usually the cold water rising main and this is the one on which condensation is most likely to occur.

Condensation. Condensation from the atmosphere is a frequent cause of damp walls and ceilings. The atmosphere contains a certain amount of moisture in the form of water vapour. The quantity varies according to the temperature of the air. Warm air can hold a greater quantity than cold. Thus, if there is a sudden temperature drop in a room which has been heated, the capacity of the air to hold moisture decreases and a point is reached when the air becomes saturated. This is known as the *dew point* and any cooling below this temperature results in condensation. The air has become saturated and the water vapour turns to liquid water.

Condensation can occur in a heated room. It shows on the walls, particularly if their surface is non-absorbent, the windows, and the ceiling (if it is a flat roof). This is because the temperature of the air at the wall or ceiling surface is considerably below that of the room air and, as the heated air in the room comes into contact with the walls or ceiling, its temperature drops abruptly and condensation forms.

As mentioned earlier in this chapter (page 43) a method of treating damp walls due to condensation is to apply a dry lining. This treatment should be considered, particularly if other causes of damp are present, such as rain penetration or rising damp.

Other causes. If your house has parapet walls and the dampcourse is defective, water may enter and form damp patches on the internal surface of the wall. It may not be possible to discern where the fault lies without obtaining expert advice. As a guide, however, the trouble is quite often due to the absence of a dampcourse immediately beneath the parapet coping. The result is that rainwater penetrates the coping and permeates down through the brickwork to form a damp patch or patches on the internal surface of the wall. Alternatively the damp patch may appear on the ceiling, particularly if the roof construction is of concrete.

Efflorescence

Efflorescence appears in the form of a white deposit on the surface of the brickwork. It is due to the migration to the surface of water-soluble salts in the bricks or in the mortar or background materials with which the bricks are associated. The salts are deposited on the surface as the moisture in the brickwork evaporates. In new work this is not likely to be serious although it may be unsightly. There is a large quantity of water used in building and until this has thoroughly dried out efflorescence may appear. The only treatment is to keep brushing the surface deposit away as it appears from time to time until it no longer reappears. In older buildings the repeated appearance of efflorescence generally means that moisture or damp is penetrating the wall for some other reason (e.g. driving rain, rising damp). If this is found to be the case and is remedied, efflorescence should not reappear. In a parapet without a dampcourse under the coping, moisture penetrating downwards can cause efflorescence. The insertion of a dampcourse should cure both the damp patches and the efflorescence.

Apart from salts inherent in the brickwork or mortar, salts may be introduced from soil in contact with the brickwork, from sea spray, or from the effect of atmospheric pollution of other materials such as limestone (e.g. sills or copings). If any of these causes are present it may be advisable to apply a protective treatment to the external surface of the wall, such as tiles or slates 'hung' on the wall or render. These are described on pages 41 and 42.

Crystallization of the salts just below the surface can lead to severe surface decay and disintegration. If individual bricks are extensively damaged they should be cut out and replaced.

Sulphate attack on mortar and rendering

Sulphates in clay bricks may cause spalling of the edges of the bricks. Alternatively the sulphates may attack the mortar causing it to expand, which in turn leads to deformation and cracking of the brickwork. If the wall is rendered externally, sulphate attack can cause extensive cracking of the render in a 'crocodile' pattern.

In severe cases there may be risk to the stability of the wall and expert advice should be sought. The process is slow, however, and only occurs when the brickwork remains wet over long periods, as in parapets, free-standing walls, and retaining walls.

If sulphate attack has caused extensive damage, however, the only cure may be to reconstruct the affected wall or sections of wall using sulphate-resisting cement. If damage has not gone too far such drastic treatment may not be necessary. In the case of a rendered wall, for example, it may be possible to render it again using sulphate-resisting cement. All cracked and non-adhering render should be hacked off, the brickwork allowed to dry, and all loose material and efflorescence removed by brushing. The wall may then be re-rendered as described on page 42.

When the wetness of the wall is due to rain penetration or rising damp and suitable remedial treatment is carried out, it should be possible to reduce or eliminate sulphate attack.

Shrinkage during drying out

Cracks occurring in brickwork are not necessarily due to movement of the foundation soil. Unfortunately it is not always a simple matter to diagnose whether cracks are due to settlement or to less serious causes such as shrinkage in new brickwork during drying out. It should be noted, however, that shrinkage cracking does not occur in clay bricks.

Shrinkage cracks may appear as a step-like crack following the horizontal and vertical joints, or as vertical cracks through brick and joint. They have certain characteristics. In uninterrupted walls they are fairly regularly spaced and uniform in width. They occur most often in concrete and sand-lime bricks. They seldom extend below the dampcourse. There is no distortion or expansion of the brickwork. The cracks develop during the first long period of dry weather after erection or in work situated in dry positions such as internal walls and the inner skins of cavity walls.

Shrinkage cracks may be unsightly but they seldom are serious. They can be repaired by cutting out the cracked bricks with a bricklayer's hammer and chisel and pointing the whole of the brickwork with a cement-lime mortar comprising one part cement, two parts lime, and nine parts well-graded sand by volume. The work should be carried out after a spell of dry weather when the brickwork is dry.

Foundation movement

Cracks due to foundation movement may be more serious and if there is any doubt as to their cause, particularly if they are noticeably worsening, expert advice should be obtained.

Where filling material has been used below the foundations and it has not been consolidated, movement may occur. Foundations on shrinkable clays may be subject to movement because of the seasonal fluctuations of the moisture content of the subsoil. Near fast-growing trees the drying effect of the roots increases the shrinkage in the soil, also affecting the clay to much greater depths.

If the foundations are considered to be inadequate then underpinning will be necessary. This involves extending the foundations below their existing level to a level below the strata of shrinkable or unstable soil. The operation is costly and only short sections are done at a time. The existing foundations are exposed for a length of say 3 ft and the soil excavated to the new depth. A concrete strip footing is then poured and brickwork built up to the underside of the existing footing. This is filled in, the next section exposed, and so on.

Corrosion of iron and steel

The corrosion of iron or steel embedded in brickwork may result in: (*a*) staining of the brickwork by rust; (*b*) corrosion at the point where a partially embedded member enters the brickwork causing cracking, or (*c*) opening of the mortar joints or cracking of the bricks. The first two are fairly easy to detect but in the case of the third it may be necessary to open up a section of brickwork surrounding the metal and expose it.

The remedy is to cut away the brickwork, in sections if necessary, expose the metal, clean it thoroughly, prime it with a rust-inhibitive primer, and paint with a bitumen paint. When rebuilding the brickwork try to ensure that the metal has a cover of dense cement mortar at least 1 in. thick. Where only part of a metal member is embedded care should be taken to protect it where it enters the brickwork and the socket should be caulked with a bituminous compound at the point of entry. If rusting of hoop iron or steel rods embedded in mortar joints is detected at an early stage the rate of corrosion can be reduced by re-pointing the brickwork joints (see p. 39).

CHAPTER 4

Doors, windows, and joinery

Even in brick houses a good deal of the structure and finish is timber. It is either structural, in the form of joists, rafters, beams, and so on, which are unplaned and usually not visible, or it is joinery timber. This includes timber doors and windows, as well as cupboards, stairs, skirtings, architraves, picture rails, and panelling.

Most solid timber used in housing is softwood and is usually painted, although inside the house this is done, not so much to protect it, as to improve its appearance. Softwood which has been carefully chosen can be treated with a clear finish (see chapter 14) and is quite decorative. Hardwood, because of the character of its natural appearance, is not usually painted, although painted hardwood is not uncommon in old houses, built at a time when hardwoods were more lavishly used in house building.

All timber moves, that is to say it expands and contracts with changes in humidity and temperature. If it was properly seasoned before use and if the joinery specification and design took account of this factor when the house was built, such movement should not be obvious or cause trouble.

Timber is susceptible to attack by certain insects and to fungal attack in the form of wet or dry rot. This is discussed in chapter 15.

At one time solid timber was extensively used for joinery. Today there is a wide range of building boards available which can be used instead. Building boards are cheaper and, if sensibly used within their limitations, every bit as satisfactory.

Doors

Pre-war houses commonly had *panelled* timber doors. These comprise a frame of solid timber with glued joints and infilling panels of thin sheets of solid timber or plywood. Infilling panels can also be of glass. In a modern house a panelled door of this type is not usual for internal doors, although this construction is used for glazed doors.

Another form of solid timber door is the *ledged and braced* type, sometimes used for low-cost external doors.

Most internal doors are today of the *flush* type. These are either *hollow core*, constructed with a softwood frame and a facing of plywood or hardboard with a hardwood lipping to protect the edges, or *solid core*, comprising a thick blockboard core faced with

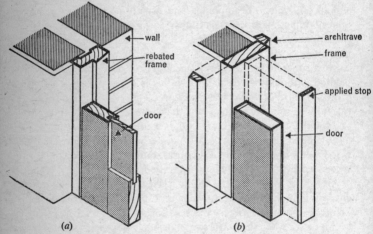

(a)   (b)

Fig. 20. Types of door frame (a) solid rebated; (b) frame with applied stop

plywood and with a hardwood lipping. A *hollow core* door is cheaper and lighter in weight than a *solid core* door but obviously not so robust.

In the case of external doors, the door frame is usually a solid piece of timber rebated to house the door. For internal doors, the frame is usually only a lining of solid timber with the rebate formed by an applied *stop* (see fig. 20).

Defects and remedies. A door may stick because it has *sagged* at the joints. Sagging is generally the result of poor workmanship or design and occurs mostly in ledged and braced doors. The edges which are sticking can be planed but this will still leave a gap at the opposite edge, which may not be acceptable. Not only does it look unsightly but it is a source of draughts. If the joints are loose the simplest remedy is probably to screw an additional brace to the door. A door may also stick at the threshold because it has *dropped* at the hinges. If the hinges are worn out this will be remedied by replacing them. Alternatively the fault may be due to the screws in the hinges working loose. They should be tightened with a screw-driver. If this proves ineffective there are two courses of action. Either replace the screws with longer ones which will 'bite' into fresh wood or, if the lining of the door is too thin, fill the holes with a patent filler and drill fresh holes. It should not be necessary to alter the position of the hinges although the problem can be over-come by doing this.

Another cause of sticking is excessive movement of the timber. The remedy is to plane off the edge or edges which stick.

Doors which do not close reasonably tightly but leave a gap are a source of draught. The draught stripping of doors is described in chapter 10.

Timber windows

Casement sashes. These are hinged like doors and have a *fastener* which secures the sash when shut and a *stay* which holds it in position when open.

Defects and remedies. A casement sash will stick just as a door does and usually for the same reasons. If the sticking is due to sagging at the joints the only effective remedy usually is to have a new sash made. If, however, it is due to the hinges or to movement of the timber it can be cured as described for doors above.

Double hung sashes. These are vertically sliding sashes usually operating in pairs. They are attached by cord or chain over pulleys to weights which run up and down within the frame of the window and are balanced so that they will stay open in any position. A catch fastens the two sashes together when closed. There is a type of patent sash balance which does not involve the use of weights or cords. It is very effective when fitted to a new window but fitting to an existing window is not easy and requires some skill.

Defects and remedies. The most common defect with a double hung window is broken or stretched sash cord. When a cord breaks it will be fairly obvious and should be repaired as soon as possible as sashes with broken cords are dangerous. A stretched cord is made apparent when the upper sash will not go right up. In this case the weight is hitting the bottom.

The procedure for replacing sash cord is as follows (fig. 21). From inside the house first remove the side bead by prising it out carefully with a screwdriver. When the nails holding this bead have been forced out and removed with pincers, the bead will have to be sprung out of position because it is held by the mitres at either end. The sash will still be held by the sound cord on the other side so it must be swung inward into the room and rested on a box or chair. The parting bead should then be removed. It is not, or should not, be tacked in position, so that its removal will not normally be unduly difficult. It may be a little obstinate due to the gluing effect of layers of paint.

Removal of the sash and beads should reveal the *pocket piece* which is a small removable section of the frame which, when unscrewed and taken out, enables the weight to be removed from behind the frame. If the pocket piece is hidden under layers of paint it is, of course, necessary to prod and scrape until you locate it. Withdraw the weight and untie the broken end of cord. The cord is attached at the other end to the sash where it is tacked in position in a groove. Remove this length and, laying it end to end with the other broken section, you will be able to measure off the length of new cord required. Tie one end of a piece of stout string to a short length of lead and the other end to the new sash cord. The length of string must equal the distance from the pulley to the pocket piece. Pass the lead over the pulley and allow it to drop down until it can be pulled through the opening for the pocket piece at the bottom. As you pull it through be careful to hold the other end of the sash cord. The cord can then be guided over the pulley and pulled down to and through the pocket piece opening. Thread this end through the hole in the sash weight and knot it securely. Holding the cord taut at the other end, fit the weight back into the pocket. Pull the weight up to the pulley and then let it slip back a little way. When this has been done hold it in place temporarily by driving a nail through the exposed cord into the frame just below

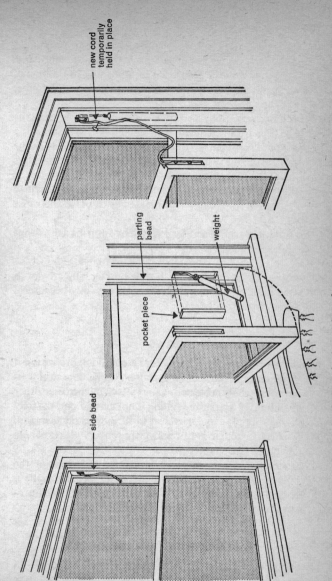

Fig. 21. Replacing a broken sash cord

the pulley. Take the free end of the cord and nail it firmly into the groove in the sash. Screw the pocket piece back into place, re-fit the parting bead, ease the sash back into position in the frame, remove the nail temporarily holding the sash cord to the frame, and replace the side bead.

Double hung sashes may also stick. This may occur because the sashes have been freshly painted. When painting new sashes it is a good idea not to paint the top of the top sash rail, merely to prime it, as this will avoid the sash sticking when closed. If sticking is due to swelling of the timber, the edges can be planed. To remove the sash to do this, it is necessary to take off the beads as described above. Sash cords should never be painted as this also will cause sticking.

Squeaking sashes can generally be cured by applying a few drops of oil to the sash pulleys.

Sliding sashes. Timber sashes which slide horizontally are not as common as casement or double hung sashes mainly because of their tendency to stick.

Metal windows

Metal windows are usually either steel or aluminium. Bronze is not common in houses because of its expense. At one time steel windows were not specially protected against attack by corrosion other than by painting. If regular repainting is not carried out, the steel is likely to rust. Simply to paint over rust will not prevent its spread. The only effective course is to remove thoroughly all rust spots before repainting (see chapter 14).

Today steel windows are given protective treatment at the factory either by the application of a zinc coating, by metallization, by hot or cold galvanizing, or by Sherardizing, all of which processes are covered by British Standard Specification.

Glazing windows and doors

Most windows are glazed with clear sheet glass. This is sold in various thicknesses according to the weight per square foot. It is important when re-glazing a sash to use the correct thickness of glass. When this is critical, such as in tall blocks of flats, architects use special methods of calculating the size of glass required, taking into account such factors as wind pressure. For most two-storey houses, however, the following figures provide a satisfactory rough guide to maximum areas of glass of different weights:

16 oz: 24 sq. ins.
21 oz: 30 sq. ins.
26 oz: 36 sq. ins.
32 oz: 40 sq. ins.

Doors and large windows are glazed with plate glass which is usually $\frac{3}{16}$ in., $\frac{1}{4}$ in., or $\frac{3}{8}$ in. thick.

The procedure for replacing a broken pane of glass in a timber window is as follows (fig. 22). First hack out the old putty using an

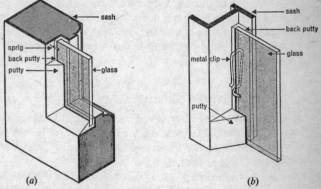

Fig. 22. Glazing a window (*a*) timber sash; (*b*) metal sash

old chisel and a mallet. Be careful not to gouge into the woodwork although this is often difficult to avoid without considerable practice at the job. Brush out the sash frame and/or glazing bars carefully after the old putty and broken glass have been removed. Check that the new piece of glass will fit the opening. When measuring the sash to order the new glass it is of course important to allow a tolerance of at least $\frac{1}{16}$ in. all round. Glass that fits tightly is likely to crack with subsequent movement of the timber frame. Run a thin ribbon of putty around the rebated face of the sash frame (known as back puttying). The new glass should then be pressed firmly but gently against this. Tack sprigs (small headless tacks) into position in front of the glass. Run putty over the sprigs between glass and frame. Using a putty knife, smooth off the exposed face of the putty and remove excess putty.

Glass in doors is usually fixed with timber glazing beads. These must be carefully prised off to remove the broken glass. Both the face of the rebated frame and the face of the bead in contact with the glass should have a ribbon of putty fixed against them before the new glass is fitted and the glazing beads refixed.

The procedure for reglazing a metal sash differs slightly (fig. 22). The broken glass and the old putty are removed in a similar way. The frame should be back puttied in the same way. Do not use ordinary glazier's putty for metal windows as the metal will not absorb the oil from the putty, hence the putty will not harden. A quick-setting putty or glazing compound suitable for metal windows should be used. The glass is not held in place with sprigs as in a timber frame. Bent clips can be used if holes have been provided in the frame. Final puttying is done in the same way as for timber windows.

Double glazing

As its name suggests, double glazing means using two sheets of glass parallel to each other where normally there is only one. It may take the form of the two sheets of glass fitted in one frame or of each fitted in a frame of its own.

Glass has a high thermal transmittance value and for this reason the amount of heat lost through the fabric of the house per square foot of surface area tends to be greatest at the windows.

In a modern house with large areas of glass, such as window walls, the expense of double glazing may well be cancelled out by the subsequent saving in fuel bills. In an older or more conventional house with smaller windows it may be difficult to justify the capital cost of double glazing on economic grounds. But in either case double glazing would be justified in terms of an improvement in the comfort conditions within the house in cold weather.

Door and window ironmongery

The term *ironmongery* is used in the building industry to denote locks, catches, fasteners, handles, and all the fittings attached to doors and windows for the purpose of opening or shutting them, locking them, and generally operating them. For the efficient functioning of doors and windows in the house it is commonsense periodically to check all ironmongery, tighten screws, oil hinges and locks.

Types of door lock. Although there is a bewildering variety of locks and latches on the market there are, basically four main types.

Latch. This is the type which does not have a key and cannot therefore be locked. It is simply a means of securing a door in the closed position. It has a spring bolt and is operated by a handle on both sides.

Dead lock. This has a single bolt which is shot and withdrawn by means of a key from either side.

Two-bolt lock. This is a combination latch and dead lock. It has a spring bolt operated by handles and a dead bolt for operation by key.

Night latch. This has a spring bolt operated by a key from the outside and knob inside. It is commonly used on front doors as it can only be opened from the outside with a key. The lock has a push button, thumb slide, or similar attachment to hold the bolt in or out.

These basic types sub-divide in turn according to the method of fixing.

Rim lock. This is the type which is fixed to the inside face of the door and requires no housing or morticing into the door. The staple (that part into which the bolt shoots to fasten the door) is attached to the frame.

Mortice lock. As its name implies this is a type which is fitted into a mortice formed in the door (fig. 23).

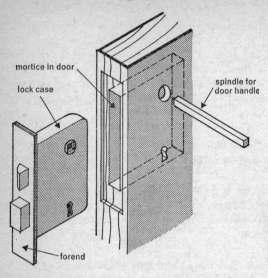

Fig. 23. Installing a mortice lock

Knobset. This is a form of mortice lock in which the lock is operated by key through the knob handle. It can also be used as a latch.

Cupboard lock. This is a type of lock used on drawers and cupboard doors. Part of the drawer or door is cut away and the lock recessed into it so that it finishes flush with the inner face.

There are, of course, many variations of these types.

Lock mechanisms. The degree of security obtained with a lock depends upon the mechanism.

Wards. These are fixed obstructions, soldered to the inside of the lock case. The key can only operate the lock if it is shaped to pass the wards. It is not a particularly effective means of security as an intruder has only to file away the base of the key bit to make it pass the wards in any lock.

Levers. A lever is a pivoted plate fitted in the lock case and held in a down position by a spring. The lever has a shaped opening called a gate formed into it and through this a lug on the bolt passes. The action of the key raises the lever into a position which enables the lug on the bolt to slide along and shoot the bolt. It is usual for a number of levers to be superimposed one upon another; the key, when turned, lines them up so that the lug can move.

Bolt-detaining mechanisms. These may take the form of either: (*a*) a single tumbler mechanism; (*b*) a pin tumbler mechanism, or (*c*) a lever mechanism. A fourth type is the disc tumbler mechanism but this is usually found only in special purpose locks. The single tumbler mechanism is one in which the catch is lifted by the key to release the bolt. The pin tumbler mechanism is more complex and hence offers greater security. It is the mechanism used in cylinder night latches. Essentially it consists of a rotatable plug in which a keyway is cut. The key turns the plug which thus withdraws the bolt by means of a connecting bar at the end of the plug. The plug is held in position by a number of spring-loaded tumblers bearing down from the body of the cylinder into the plug. Only the correct key will match these tumblers and lift them out of the plug back into the cylinder body to enable the plug to be rotated and release the bolt. A lever mechanism has already been described above.

Care of locks. Most locks require regular attention if they are to continue to work properly. The most frequent causes of deterioration and failure are dirt and rust. An excessive build up of both or either will eventually cause the bolt in a lock to stick. If rust appears on or around the bolt, spread a good quality thin oil, such as sewing machine or typewriter oil, around the bolt. If a key squeaks or is difficult to turn, it should be oiled on the nose and the bearing. If a lock appears to be completely clogged, it will be necessary to remove it from the door and open the case, as described below, and thoroughly clean and oil the mechanism. Grease or oil should not be used on the cylinder or keys of a cylinder lock. They should be lubricated with graphite. The key can be so lubricated by rubbing it with a black lead pencil.

Defects and remedies. One of the most frequent defects in a lock or catch is a broken spring (fig. 24). This can be tested by depressing the bolt. If it fails to fly back when released, the spring is broken. To replace it the lock must be removed from the door. First remove the knobs or handles. In some types they are fixed by a small grub screw in the neck into the spindle. In others they are screwed to the door. When the handles are removed the spindle can be withdrawn. In the case of a mortice lock the exposed end of the lock is

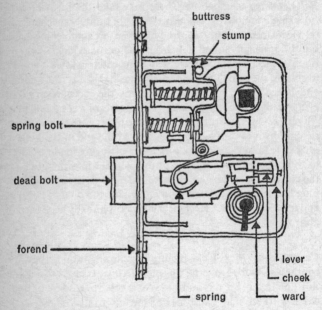

Fig. 24. Upright mortice lock (casing removed)

screwed to the edge of the door. These screws must be undone so that the lock can be eased out of the door with the help of a screwdriver. The casing of the lock must now be opened to expose the mechanism. The fractured or broken spring can then be removed and the new spring fitted into place. Take the opportunity of cleaning and oiling the mechanism before re-assembling it and fitting the lock back into the door.

Stairs

The component parts of a typical timber staircase are illustrated in fig. 25.

The most common defect arising in staircases is the creaking tread. This occurs if the tread deflects when trodden on. In well constructed stairs each tread is supported at mid-span by the

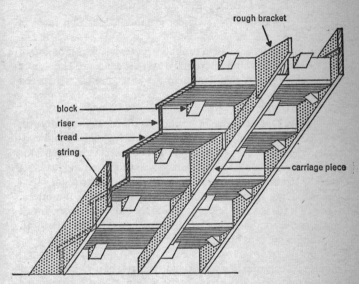

Fig. 25. Timber stair construction (view from underside)

carriage piece. If there is no carriage piece and the thickness of tread is not sufficiently stout, deflection will occur. The most effective remedy is to fit a carriage piece, attaching brackets to it and screwing through the top of each tread into the brackets. Creaking may occur because the tread, which is glued to the riser, has worked loose. A couple of screws through the tread into the riser may cure the trouble.

CHAPTER 5

Floors

Timber ground floors

Typical construction for a timber ground-floor is illustrated in chapter 3, fig. 12.

The floor joists are nailed to timber *plates* which rest on top of brick *sleeper* walls built up from the oversite concrete. The sleeper walls, which run at right angles to the joists, are usually spaced about 4 ft 6 ins. apart.

Ventilation. One of the chief hazards to timber floors is dry rot, described in chapter 15. If a floor is properly designed and constructed this problem need never arise. The air space between floor joists and oversite concrete should be well ventilated and, to assist this, the sleeper walls are built in *honeycomb* construction, which means leaving spaces between the vertical joints of the bricks. External walls have air bricks built into the outer leaf of brickwork and a corresponding space left between bricks in the inner leaf. In addition the ends of joists should be kept clear of the walls.

Damp. It is essential that a continuous barrier be provided against rising damp. This is done by laying a damp-proof course in the walls at a minimum 6 ins. above ground level (prescribed by the by-laws). A similar dampcourse is placed on top of all sleeper walls. The traditional dampcourse takes the form of two courses of slates bedded on cement mortar. Today there are many proprietary materials on the market consisting of a hessian, fibre felt, asbestos, or lead base saturated with, and sandwiched between, two layers of bitumen. Other materials less commonly used are sheet lead, sheet copper, mastic asphalt and two courses of engineering bricks laid in cement mortar.

Concrete ground floors

Concrete ground-floors are usually referred to as *solid floors*. A typical construction is illustrated in fig. 26.

It is quite usual to have a hardwood strip floor nailed to preservative-impregnated battens set in a 2-in. thick concrete screed. There

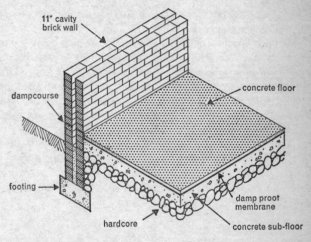

Fig. 26. Concrete ground floor construction

are many other finishes suitable for fixing to a solid floor and these are discussed on pages 73 to 84.

Damp. The question of ventilation does not arise, but the need to provide a damp-proof barrier is no less critical than with a timber floor. The damp-proof course built into the walls should form a continuous barrier with the damp-proof membrane in the floor. This membrane is placed either between two thicknesses of concrete or between the concrete and the screed on which the floor finish is laid. There are many materials used for damp proof membranes. Whilst all of them are impermeable to liquid water not all are impermeable to water vapour. Those which are completely impervious include mastic asphalt, pitch mastic, and bonded bitumen felt. Building papers and cold bitumen–water emulsions are not considered to be resistant to the passage of water vapour. Integral water-proofers are sometimes added to the concrete instead of a damp-proof membrane, but though this will render the concrete resistant to water itself, its permeability to water vapour is not materially affected. Some of the floor finishes described on pages 72 to 86 are themselves impermeable to water and vapour.

Solid ground-floors like the one illustrated are relatively new to house building in this country. There is a widespread belief that a concrete floor is cold. In fact a concrete floor which has a sound damp-proof membrane holds heat extremely well. It has a higher resistance to the transmission of heat than a timber floor. This ability to retain warmth is made use of in the type of house heating known as electric floor warming. Cables are embedded in the floor screed and heat is 'stored up' during off-peak periods. See chapter 11 for a full description.

In old houses, timber basement floors (or ground-floors if there is no basement) which have become extensively damaged by dry rot can be taken up and replaced by concrete and, provided care is taken to include an effective damp-proof membrane, a warm, dry floor will result.

Timber upper floors

The construction of timber upper floors takes the form of joists spaced at about 16 ins. from centre to centre which are supported on the walls of the house. Whilst in older houses it is not unusual to have the floor joists supported in intermediate positions by beams (which project below the ceiling), in contemporary building it is normal practice to span the joists between load-bearing walls and for this reason the joists are deeper than ground-floor joists. When the span between walls exceeds about 9 ft, *herringbone strutting* is used, rows of struts being spaced at approximately 6 ft, centre to centre. Herringbone strutting consists of small pieces of timber, usually 2 ins. × 2 ins. bridging between joists (fig. 27). Its object is to resist deflection of the joists.

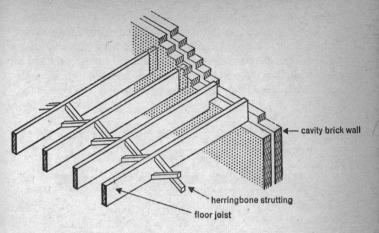

Fig. 27. Timber upper floor construction

Concrete upper floors

Concrete upper floors, still comparatively rare in houses, usually take the form of reinforced concrete slabs spanning between the walls. In multi-storey flat construction the floor slab is often placed over clay or precast concrete 'hollow pots' laid in the bottom of the formwork before concrete is poured. This type of floor is in fact supported on reinforced concrete beams (fig. 28).

An alternative method is to support the floor on a series of hollow precast concrete beams laid side by side (fig. 28). There are, of course, any number of variations of this form of construction, most of which are proprietary systems devised by construction companies and precast concrete manufacturers. The hollow pots and beams not only reduce the weight and hence the *dead load* of the building as a whole, but also provide continuous spaces through which conduits and service pipes can run.

Floor screeds

Most of the floor finishes described on the following pages are suitable for laying on a concrete base or sub-floor. To ensure satisfactory results the base must be smooth and level. Generally, the only way to achieve this is to lay a screed over the base before putting down the floor finish. This is particularly true of existing houses when a concrete surface, which has not previously had a finish on it, is likely to have been worn and damaged by traffic and, in any case, is not likely to have been laid smooth and level in the

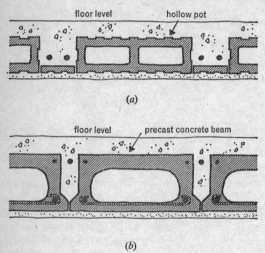

Fig. 28. Types of concrete upper floor (*a*) hollow pot; (*b*) precast concrete beam

first place. There are numerous excellent floor finishes on the market today, but many of them, thermoplastic and p.v.c. tiles, for instance, are quite thin and it is absolutely essential that the base on which they are laid is sound and level.

Proprietary levelling compounds are available and these are often obtainable from the manufacturers of the floor finishes. Most manufacturers recommend a cement screed when the condition of the concrete base calls for it, and the following is a method of laying one.

The surface of the concrete base must provide an effective key to which the screed will bond. It must, therefore, be roughened, if necessary, by chipping it with a pick. Once this is done brush the surface well as loose particles and dust left behind might affect adhesion of the screed. The concrete base should then be washed to remove dust and dirt. After washing, the whole surface should be flooded with water and left for some time before the laying of the screed.

If a screed is put on to a new concrete base which has not yet hardened it need be only $\frac{3}{4}$ in. thick. In all other cases it should be at least 1 in. thick or $1\frac{1}{2}$ ins. when placed over old floors. When a screed is to be laid over a damp-proof membrane it should be 2 ins. thick.

Having prepared the base and decided the thickness of screed it is next necessary to mark the level. The simplest way to do this is to place a 3-in. wide timber batten of the appropriate thickness around the perimeter of the room hard up against the walls. The screed will be levelled flush with the top of this batten. If the floor finish is to be wall to wall carpet, the batten will subsequently serve as a nailing strip. Never attempt to lay more than about 120 sq. ft, of screed at a time. Large floors should be divided into equal bays by means of timber battens of the same thickness as the finished screed. If the concrete base has expansion joints in it arrange the joints of the bays over these.

The most suitable mix for a screed is one part of cement to three or four parts of clean aggregate by volume. The aggregate can be sand or crushed granite graded from $\frac{3}{16}$ in. downward. The screed should be a dry mix to avoid cracking due to shrinkage as it dries out. Measure out the sand first, add the cement, and mix them together before adding water. Add just enough water to get the right consistency and mix thoroughly. Many people make the mix too wet because, that way, it is easier to spread. The screed should be placed or spread into position with a spade and a screeding board used to level it. To do this use a sawing action, placing the ends of the board on the levelling battens. If the type of floor finish necessitates a steel trowelled surface (the floor finish manufacturer will advise you) this must be done after the screed has stiffened slightly, a process which may take several hours depending on the weather and the ventilation. When laying a screed over a damp-proof membrane spread some sand on it first. This will assist adhesion.

Floor finishes: timber

(i) SOFTWOOD STRIP AND BOARD

Strip and board floorings are usually produced in tongued and grooved form, although square edge board (i.e. butt-jointed) is used extensively in domestic building mainly as a sub-floor for other finishes (e.g. carpet, linoleum).

The term *strip* is used in the timber trade to mean widths of 4 ins. or less, whereas *board* refers to widths in excess of 4 ins. Softwood flooring is usually quoted in *nominal* widths and thicknesses. This refers to the size of the timber before it is planed. The finished sizes, that is after planing, are therefore slightly less. The most common widths (nominal) for strip flooring are 3 ins. and 4 ins. For board flooring the most common width is 6 ins. (nominal). The most common thicknesses for both strip and board are 1 in. and $1\frac{1}{4}$ ins. (nominal).

Types of softwood. Timbers suitable for use when exposed are Douglas fir (Oregon pine), pitch pine, western hemlock, redwood. Softwoods which are recommended only as a sub-floor are deal and European whitewood.

The base. Softwood flooring is usually nailed direct into the floor joists with 2-in. oval wire nails. The heads should be punched below floor level.

Maintenance. A softwood floor which is to be left exposed should be carefully maintained. After laying, the floor should be sanded and treated with a good quality floor seal.

(ii) HARDWOOD STRIP

Hardwood strip flooring, produced in tongued and grooved form, may be fixed direct to timber joists or, in the case of a concrete sub-floor, to treated softwood battens cast in the concrete or fixed on top of the concrete by means of proprietary metal clips.

Strip is produced in lengths usually not less than about 3 ft. Most common widths (nominal) are 2 ins., $2\frac{1}{2}$ ins., 3 ins., $3\frac{1}{2}$ ins., and 4 ins. and thicknesses (nominal) $\frac{7}{8}$ in. and 1 in. Unlike softwood, hardwood strip is often secret nailed, so that nail heads are invisible on the finished floor.

Battens should be spaced from 12 to 24 ins. apart and should be not less than 2 ins. wide by 1½ ins. thick.

(iii) HARDWOOD BLOCK, PARQUET

Hardwood block flooring comprises short pieces of timber about 3½ ins. wide by 9 or 12 ins. long by 1 in. or 1¼ ins. (nominal) thick,

Fig. 29. Parquet floor patterns (*a*) square basket; (*b*) diagonal basket; (*c*) brick; (*d*) herringbone

laid in a pattern (fig. 29) and bedded in an adhesive on to a concrete sub-floor.

There is a wide variety of hardwoods available. They include beech, birch, iroko, jarrah, karri, mahogany, maple, English oak,

European oak, American oak, Tasmanian oak, Japanese oak, and teak. A number of hardwoods are on display at The Building Centre, London.

Blocks have a chamfer along the bottom of the longitudinal edges to take up surplus adhesive squeezed up during laying. They are interlocking usually by means of tongues and grooves or dowels. The adhesive on which they are laid is hot coal tar or hot or cold bitumen.

Blocks may also be laid over joists or on an existing board floor. In such cases an underlay such as resin-bonded plywood must be used. When used over joists the plywood should be $\frac{3}{8}$ in. thick for joists at 12 ins. spacing or $\frac{1}{2}$ in. for 16 ins. spacing. Joints between sheets of plywood should occur only over joists or bridging pieces between joists. Nails or screws should be fixed not less than $\frac{1}{4}$ in. from the edge of the sheets and at 12-in. centres and screws should be at least $\frac{1}{2}$ in. larger than the thickness of the plywood. When laid over an existing board floor, $\frac{1}{8}$-in. thick plywood is satisfactory.

Parquet flooring consists of much smaller pieces of wood, usually only about $\frac{1}{4}$ in. thick and laid on an underlay. The laying of hardwood block and parquet floors is a job for specialists. Names of firms who carry out this work may be obtained from The Building Centre, London, and the Timber Research and Development Association.

There are a number of proprietary forms of block and parquet flooring, information concerning which can be obtained from the above organizations and, in addition, from the British Institute of Hardwood Flooring Specialists. The Hardwood Flooring Manufacturers' Association can supply names of manufacturers of particular species of hardwood strip and block flooring and the Association of Flooring Contractors can supply regional lists of specialist contractors.

Linoleum

Linoleum is produced on a backing of either hessian, to British Standard B.S.810, or bitumen-impregnated paper-felt, known as felt-backed, to B.S.1863. Felt-backed linoleum was originally produced in this country because of a shortage of hessian, but production has continued owing to its lower price. Linoleum is manufactured in a range of thicknesses measured in millimetres (mm.) and it is advisable, when purchasing, to specify the required thickness. The following table gives thicknesses of various types of linoleum. Needless to say not every manufacturer makes every type, nor is each colour pattern available in every thickness.

Thicknesses of different types of linoleum (in mm.)

Plain and marble	Moire and Jaspe	Inlaid	Felt-backed plain, marble, Moire, Jaspe
6·7	6·7	4·5	3·2
6·0	4·5	3·2	2·5
(plain only)			
4·5	3·2	2·0	
3·2	2·5*	1·6	
2·5	2·0		
2·0	1·6		

In most houses 3·2 mm. thickness or less is adequate.

* Not listed in B.S.810 and B.S.1863.

The base. Although linoleum is a flexible material it gives best service when laid on a firm base. For this reason a tongued and grooved timber floor is more suitable than a square edge one. All nail heads should be punched down, irregularities planed or sanded off, and holes filled with plaster, plastic wood, or a similar filler. Concrete is an admirable base for linoleum but manufacturers advise that the best results are obtained if a 1-in. thick screed, comprising one part Portland cement to three parts sand, is first laid on the concrete. In the case of a solid ground-floor, an adequate damp-proof membrane must be provided.

Laying. If it is proposed to lay linoleum on a very worn timber floor, it is advisable to use an underlay of 4-mm. plywood or ⅛-in. hardboard sheets on the floor as a base for the new linoleum. Sheets should be close-butted with their joints staggered and they should be secured with flat-headed screw nails with 4 ins. between centres in both directions. On a concrete surface which is very uneven it is necessary to bring the surface up to level with the use of a levelling compound such as latex cement.

On timber floors it is quite usual to lay linoleum loose. It must be remembered, however, that the linoleum will expand and provision must be made for this when laying. It should not be cut to fit too closely against the skirting, for example, and when two widths meet they should be left with one overlapping the other until expansion has stopped, and then cut to fit.

If linoleum is stuck down to the timber floor there is no need to wait for expansion to occur as the adhesive restrains movement. As mentioned above it is best to use an underlay of resin-bonded plywood or hardboard in such cases. A cheaper alternative is to stick a linoleum underfelt to the timber boards and stick the linoleum to the underfelt. The joints between sheets of linoleum should be at right angles to the joints between sheets of underfelt. Linoleum underfelts, 6 ft wide, are either plain (grey) or bitumen-saturated (black) paper felts. It is not advisable to stick linoleum only around the edges and in the middle.

There are several types of adhesive on the market, including vegetable and casein glue types, lignum pastes, gum-spirit adhesives, bitumen-rubber emulsions, and bitumen-rubber solutions. It is advisable to consult the linoleum manufacturer or supplier and use his proprietary adhesive, if one is available. The solvent used in spirit-based adhesives, for example, can have the effect of softening the bitumen in underlays or damp-proof membranes.

LINOLEUM TILES

Linoleum, particularly in the thicker grades, is also available in tile form. The technique of setting out and laying is the same as for thermoplastic tiles. In the thicker grades (6·0 mm. and 6·7 mm.) it is customary to remove the hessian backing before laying the tiles. Manufacturers make a material with a lightly attached hessian for this purpose.

Maintenance. Linoleum should be washed with warm water and mild detergent when necessary. Alkaline or abrasive cleaners are harmful and a scrubbing brush should not be used. After washing and when it has dried thoroughly, the linoleum should be given two thin coats of emulsion polish. Frequency of polishing will depend on the amount of traffic a floor gets. If applied too often a thick layer soon builds up and collects dirt and dust. For floors which do not get much traffic an application of polish every 3 to 6 weeks is adequate. For moderate traffic polish should be applied every 1 to 3 weeks. The floor may require washing occasionally with a wet mop but detergents should not be used or the polish will be removed. If the floor receives a lot of traffic, dirt becomes ingrained in the polish and it will be necessary to wash the floor with detergent or white spirit to remove the dirt and, incidentally, the polish. Fresh polish must then be applied.

Thermoplastic tiles

Thermoplastic tiles are manufactured from thermoplastic-resin binders, fluxes, short-fibre asbestos, powdered mineral filler, and pigments. Tiles are usually 9 ins. × 9 ins. but 6 ins. × 6 ins. and 12 ins. × 12 ins. are also available. Thickness is usually $\frac{1}{8}$ in., sometimes $\frac{3}{16}$ in. A variety of plain colours and marbled patterns is available. Dark colours cost less because the dark resin binders are cheapest. The tiles are brittle and may be broken by hand but once laid on a flat rigid base this is not a disadvantage. The technique of setting out and laying is similar to that of linoleum tiles.

The base. If the base is timber floorboards it is advisable to provide an underlay of hardboard or resin-bonded plywood. A concrete base floor should have a smooth finished screed on which to lay the tiles. The screed should be at least 1 in. thick and composed of one part of Portland cement to 3 to 4 parts clean sand.

Laying. The base floor should be swept clean before laying tiles. Tiles should be laid starting in the centre of the room. To find the centre stretch a chalked string between nails driven into the floor against the end walls. Stretch the string tightly between the nails, then lift it and allow it to drop back to the floor, thus marking a chalk line on the floor. Double the string to get the centre point.

Lay two tiles side by side on each side of the centre line immediately to the right of the centre point. Draw a pencil line along the side of the tiles, forming a right angle with the first chalk line at the centre point. Remove the tiles. Make a chalk line over the pencil line using the chalked string and nails as before.

On a concrete base floor a priming coat of adhesive should be applied. When this is completely dry (usually 1–1½ hours, depending on the weather) laying can commence. Spread enough adhesive to take a maximum of 16 tiles. Whilst the adhesive is still tacky lay the first tile in the angle of the chalk lines. Subsequent tiles should be lowered, *not* slid into position, and pressure applied firmly and evenly. Sliding the tiles causes adhesive to ooze out. Few walls are completely straight and it will be necessary to cut each tile separ-

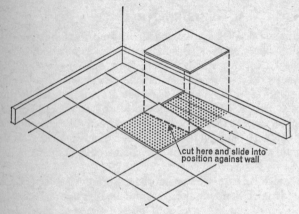

cut here and slide into
position against wall

Fig. 30. Cutting linoleum or thermoplastic tiles at walls

ately at the walls. To do this first lay a tile loose exactly on top of a tile in the last row. Place a second tile on top of this, but abutting the wall, and use the edge of this as a guide to mark the first tile (fig. 30).

Tiles may be used on the risers and treads of stairs but they cannot satisfactorily be bent round the nose of a step and a pre-formed nosing must be used. Tiles may be bent to form a cove but it must be a large radius cove and the tile must be fully supported. This means that in the case of a screeded floor the screed must be coved. For laying tiles use an adhesive recommended or supplied by the manufacturer and follow his instructions carefully.

Maintenance. A thermoplastic tile floor may be walked on immediately. The floor should not be washed for about two weeks after laying. It should be kept clean by brushing with a soft broom. After this it may be washed with warm water and soap or mild detergent. To remove stains, the surface should be rubbed lightly with a fine steel wool dipped in scouring powder. Do not use paraffin or petrol as they will soften the resin binding agent of the tile and cause disintegration. If a polished surface is required a water-wax emulsion polish should be used. Paste polishes contain turpentine or white spirit which soften the tiles.

P.V.C. sheet and tiles, thermoplastic vinyl tiles

Polyvinyl chloride resin is a snow-white, brittle resin which softens when heated. In this form it is quite unsuitable for flooring. It is mixed with plasticizers, therefore, to form a rubber-like material which is the basis of P.V.C. floor finishes. The finished form of flooring may be of the following basic types: P.V.C. sheet or tile, fabric-backed P.V.C. sheet or tile, and thermoplastic vinyl tile.

P.V.C. sheet is usually manufactured 36 or 54 ins. wide and tiles 9 ins. × 9 ins. or 12 ins. × 12 ins. Both sheet and tile can be made in a variety of clean, bright colours and marble effects. As a flooring it is similar to rubber; it has probably slightly lower resistance to wear but much greater resistance to grease and solvents.

Two main types of fabric-backed P.V.C. flooring are made. One type is manufactured from a mixture of plasticized P.V.C. fillers and pigments which is fed, while hot, on to a hessian backing and passed between heated rollers. The sheet thus formed is kept hot for some time to remove strains and is then rolled up. The process is basically similar to linoleum manufacture except that no 'stoving' is needed. Sheet is made 72 ins. wide and 2 mm. thick in plain colours and marble patterns.

The other type is more flexible, contains little filler, and is made by a rather different process. P.V.C., plasticizer, and pigments are mixed while cold to give a paste which is spread by roller or knife on to a moving sheet of fabric. The sheet then passes through a hot zone in which the paste is converted to a tough film. The material is made in sheets up to 65 ins. wide and up to $\frac{1}{8}$ in. thick. Plain colours are available but not marble finishes. Either hessian or upholstery felt is used for backing; the hessian-backed material is intended to be stuck, the felt type to be laid loose.

Thermoplastic vinyl tiles are made from a mixture of plasticized P.V.C., asbestos, limestone, and pigment. They are available in a wide range of colours and, unlike thermoplastic tiles, price bears no relation to colour. Tiles can be made in sizes larger than thermoplastic tiles but 9 ins. × 9 ins. is the most common size. They are more expensive than the equivalent thickness of thermoplastic tiles but anyway can be used less thick than thermoplastic. Tiles as thin as $\frac{1}{16}$ in. are available but require a very smooth and even sub-floor.

The base. A concrete sub-floor should have a smooth screed finish as described for thermoplastic tiles. P.V.C. sheet and tiles expand considerably when wetted and should not, therefore, be laid on a concrete ground-floor which has not got a damp-proof membrane. Also, when laying on a new screed it is essential that a thorough drying out period of at least 2 to 3 weeks be allowed for the screed before laying the P.V.C. Fabric-backed P.V.C. finishes behave in the same way and the above precautions should be observed. Thermoplastic vinyl tiles are much less sensitive to moisture, but they should not be used as a damp-proof barrier.

Timber floors are a suitable base for P.V.C., fabric-backed P.V.C., and thermoplastic vinyl provided the surface is even and nail heads are punched down. Slight movements of the boards will not cause cracking. It is always important when putting finishes of this type on a timber sub-floor to ensure that the underside of the timber is well ventilated, otherwise dry rot may occur. For this reason these finishes should not be put on wood blocks on a concrete ground-floor.

Clay or concrete tiles provide a suitable base, but as with concrete there must be a damp-proof membrane. If the tiles are very uneven a thin screeding of rubber latex, cement, and sand, or of a bitumen emulsion, cement, and sand should be applied.

Smooth mastic asphalt or pitch mastic is also a suitable base but the adhesive for sticking the floor finish must be of a type that does not soften asphalt or pitch. The adhesive manufacturer should be consulted.

P.V.C. and thermoplastic vinyl finishes may be laid on a magnesite sub-floor provided there is a damp-proof membrane when the magnesite is on a concrete ground-floor.

Laying. The base should be dry and clean. All grit, dirt, oil, grease, etc. should be removed. P.V.C. sheet and tile are laid in much the same way as rubber. The base and the underside of the P.V.C. are each coated with a thin layer of adhesive. When both are tacky the P.V.C. is placed in position and pressed down.

Fabric-backed P.V.C. sheet and tiles are laid in a similar way to linoleum (p. 74), and thermoplastic vinyl to thermoplastic (p. 77).

Any of these finishes is suitable for covering the risers and treads of stairs, but a preformed nosing of rubber, metal, or P.V.C. should be used. Only thermoplastic vinyl are suitable for forming into a coved skirting and, even then, only if the cove is of large radius and the tiles are fully supported (i.e. by forming the cove in the screed). It is better to use a preformed coving piece to match the tiles or sheet.

Maintenance. All of these finishes can take traffic very soon after laying. They can be washed with soap and water. Oil or grease marks can be removed with petrol or white spirit. If desired paste or emulsion polishes may be applied.

Terrazzo

Terrazzo is basically a form of concrete comprising usually a coloured cement and a very hard aggregate such as marble. It may take the form of precast tiles, usually 6, 9, 12, 18, or 24 ins. square, or it may be cast *in situ*. It is a finish which should only be laid by specialist firms employing skilled labour.

The base. Tiles are normally laid direct on to a concrete sub-floor. *In situ* terrazzo is laid on a $1\frac{1}{2}$-in. thick screed on a concrete sub-floor.

Laying. Tiles are bedded on the sub-floor in a 3:1 sand and cement mix. The thickness of the bedding is from $\frac{1}{2}$ in. to 1 in. according to the size of the tile. *In situ* terrazzo is laid to a thickness of $\frac{1}{2}$ in. to $\frac{5}{8}$ in. on the screed and is divided into squares by means of metal, ebonite, or plastic strips to avoid shrinkage cracks. When the terrazzo has set, the surface is finished by rubbing it down with abrasive stone to expose and polish the aggregate.

Maintenance. Terrazzo is a hard-wearing surface which is easily cleaned with non-caustic cleaner and the occasional use of a scouring powder. It should not be washed with normal soaps as these tend to make the surface slippery.

Quarry tiles

Quarry tiles are made from ordinary clays or unrefined clays and are manufactured mostly in Staffordshire and North Wales where the clays are found. They are available in blues, reds, browns, and buffs, and standard sizes (B.S.1286:1945) are 4 ins. × 4 ins. × $\frac{3}{4}$ in. thick, 6 ins. × 6 ins. × $\frac{5}{8}$ in. and $\frac{7}{8}$ in., and 9 ins. × 9 ins. × $1\frac{1}{4}$ ins. Other sizes also available are 8 ins. × 8 ins. × $1\frac{1}{8}$ ins., 9 ins. × 9 ins. × $1\frac{1}{2}$ ins., and 12 ins. × 12 ins. × $1\frac{1}{2}$ ins. and 2 ins. Coves and internal and external angles are produced.

The base. Quarry tiles are laid on a concrete base, preferably on a $\frac{3}{4}$-in. thick screed, comprising 1 part cement to 3 parts sand.

Laying. Tiles should be soaked in clean water before laying. They should be laid whilst the screed is still green on a $\frac{1}{4}$-in. thick bed comprising 1 part cement to 3 parts sand. A wide joint ($\frac{1}{8}$ in.) should be left between tiles and the usual way to grout this joint is by brushing a creamy paste of cement mortar (1:1 cement and sand) across the tiles. The surface should be cleaned immediately with sand or sawdust. The floor should not be walked upon for 4 or 5 days.

Maintenance. As soon as possible after the tiles are laid linseed oil should be applied. It should be well rubbed in and not flooded on. Thereafter the only maintenance necessary is regular washing with clean water and soft soap.

Plain clay tiles

Plain clay floor tiles are made from refined natural clay. Standard sizes are 3 ins. × 3 ins., 4 ins. × 4 ins., $4\frac{1}{4}$ ins. × $4\frac{1}{4}$ ins., and 6 ins. × 6 ins., all $\frac{1}{2}$ in. thick, and standard coves, skirtings, and other fittings are available. They are made in a variety of colours and surface finishes are smooth, ribbed, grooved, or studded.

These tiles are laid and maintained in the same way as quarry tiles.

Cork tiles

Tiles made from granulated cork or cork shavings are available in thicknesses from $\frac{1}{4}$ in. to $\frac{9}{16}$ in. ($\frac{5}{16}$ in. is the most common) and in sizes up to 36 ins. × 12 ins., the most usual being 12 ins. × 12 ins. Two qualities are available, ordinary and heavy density, either with a tongue and groove or a straight edge.

The base. Cork tiles may be laid on a timber sub-floor or a concrete base. In the latter case they should be laid on 3 : 1 sand and cement screed, given a steel trowelled finish.

Laying. Fixing to a timber sub-floor is by means of panel pins nailed through the corners of the tile. When laid on a screed they should be bedded in a bitumen adhesive.

Maintenance. Cork floors should be polished with a liquid wax emulsion. They should *not* be washed often.

Rubber

Rubber is available in sheet and tile form. Sheet rubber is either of the type which is of similar material throughout its thickness or comprises a thin surfacing mounted on a foam rubber backing. It is manufactured in thicknesses of $\frac{1}{8}$ in., $\frac{3}{16}$ in., and $\frac{1}{4}$ in. in rolls 42 ins. wide and from 50 ft to 100 ft long.

The base. Rubber can be laid on a timber or concrete base, provided the surface is even, level, and free from cracks. If the sub-floor is timber boarding, an underlay of hardboard or resin-bonded plywood should be provided; if laid on concrete a 3:1 sand and cement screed should be provided. If the concrete base is in direct contact with the ground a damp-proof membrane should be laid under the screed.

Laying. Rubber floors should be laid in an adhesive and the laying should be carried out by a specialist firm. Names and addresses are available from the Building Centres.

Maintenance. The floor surface should be washed with a damp cloth and ordinary household soap. It should then be dried with a soft cloth which will produce a natural, dirt-resisting polish. Detergents and abrasive soap powders should not be used.

Chipboard

Wood chipboard can be used as a floor surface laid on top of joists instead of timber boarding. Bridging pieces must be provided between the joists so that all edges of boards are supported. The usual thickness of chipboard is $\frac{3}{4}$ in. for this purpose. Standard width is 4 ft and standard length 8 ft, although longer lengths are available.

The base. Used in this form chipboard is laid direct on timber joists which should be at 16-in. centres. In this way no waste will result from using 4-ft × 8-ft sheets.

Chipboard can also be laid on a concrete floor in which timber fillets have been set at 2-ft intervals.

Laying. On a joist floor the chipboard is nailed direct into the joists and the bridging pieces with lost head nails spaced at approximately 12 ins. between centres.

Maintenance. Chipboard floors should be sealed with a floor seal. Consult the chipboard manufacturer for a suitable type. It should be cleaned by wiping with a damp cloth.

Hardboard

Sheet hardboard is often used as a base for other floor finishes such as thermoplastic tiles, linoleum, and cork when laid over existing timber floors which are in poor condition. It makes quite a satisfactory floor finish in itself, however, and when treated with a clear seal is both durable and pleasing in appearance. A thickness of $\frac{1}{8}$ in. is generally adequate although $\frac{3}{16}$ in. is better if the floor is particularly uneven, and standard hardboard is quite satisfactory for the purpose.

The base. Hardboard can be laid on an existing timber floor or on a concrete base. When laid on concrete the base surface should be smooth and level and it is advisable to put down a 1-in. thick screed.

Laying. On an existing timber floor hardboard should be fixed in position by nailing into the base floor with flat-headed screw nails spaced 4 ins. apart. Hardboard laid on a screed or concrete base should be fixed with a gum spirit or bitumen-rubber emulsion adhesive.

Maintenance. Hardboard floors should be sealed with a suitable floor seal.

Surface treatments

Floor seals. There is a wide range of floor seals on the market today. These are of several types – phenolic/drying oil sealers, alkyd/drying oil sealers, oleoresinous sealers, etc. – and they all aim to cover the floor with a transparent plastic film which at once protects it and preserves a fresh appearance. Wax may be applied on top of a seal and some manufacturers actually recommend it.

Wax. The hardest wearing waxes are those with high melting points. Because they are not readily dispersed in solvents they generally have to be applied in the form of an emulsion in water. Soft or low melting point waxes can be dispersed in organic solvents and they take the form of paste or liquid wax polishes which are applied with a rag.

Penetrating oil. This is a finish sometimes applied to timber floors. It binds the surface fibres of the wood by means of a resinous substance which prevents splintering of the surface and increases resistance to wear. As this treatment does not provide a surface seal it does not prevent dirt becoming ingrained in the surface and if the floor gets a lot of traffic it is advisable to apply a floor seal or a wax on top of the penetrating oil.

Linoleum paint. If you tire of the appearance of linoleum before it is worn out or if it has become shabby, you can paint it with linoleum paint. Special preparations are available, details of which can be obtained from the Building Centres. Before applying it, however, all dirt and polish must be removed from the linoleum. The floor should be thoroughly washed with hot water and soap, then rinsed with cold water. When this has dried, rub the floor with a piece of rag dipped in turpentine. This will remove remaining traces of polish. Once this has evaporated the linoleum can be painted. Always use the particular paint recommended for the job and follow the manufacturer's instructions faithfully.

Choice of floor finish

The appearance of a floor is, for most people, important and will be a major consideration in choice. Other factors are listed below.

For a wood joist floor, softwood (strip and board) and chipboard finishes are suitable. For a concrete base floor, terrazzo, quarry tiles, and plain clay tiles are suitable, whilst the following finishes are suitable for either floor: hardwood strip, hardwood block and parquet, linoleum, thermoplastic tiles, p.v.c. sheet and tiles, thermoplastic vinyl tiles, cork tiles, rubber, hardboard.

Cost. The cost of floor finishes varies considerably even between grades or types of a particular finish, linoleum being a good example of this. Unless the budget is extremely tight, however, cost should not be considered on its own. Some floors have a much longer life than others although they cost more in the first place.

Again, some floors have a much higher resistance to heavy wear, and so on.

Cleaning and maintenance. Hardwood and terrazzo floors require little cleaning. An average amount of cleaning can be expected with quarry tiles, plain clay tiles, softwood board and strip, chipboard, hardboard, linoleum, rubber, and p.v.c. Floors which may require special treatment include cork and thermoplastic tiles.

Resistance to wear. Floors in certain parts of the house obviously receive more wear than those in other parts. Some thought should be given to this in the choice of floor finishes throughout the house. Floors with a very high resistance to wear are hardwood, terrazzo, and p.v.c. tiles. Quarry tiles, plain clay tiles, hardboard, cork, linoleum, rubber, and thermoplastic, though not as hard wearing as hardwood and terrazzo, have a high resistance to wear.

Quietness. The quietness of a floor is generally a measure of its resilience. Cork, rubber, and p.v.c. all have high resiliences and, consequently, are quiet floors.

Resistance to rising damp. While few finishes are impervious to damp, a number are unaffected by it and are very suitable, therefore, for basement floors. They include terrazzo, quarry tiles, plain clay tiles, and thermoplastic tiles.

Underfloor heating. *In situ* terrazzo is not suitable as a finish on underfloor heating unless it is laid whilst the base concrete or screed containing the heating elements is green. Rubber is only suitable as a finish if it is entirely synthetic.

External paving

There are several materials suitable for paths and paving in the garden and around the house. Concrete cast *in situ* is the one most commonly used. The techniques of mixing and laying concrete can be fairly easily mastered by a determined handyman and the material has certain functional advantages: it is tough and hard wearing and easy to keep clean. But it must be remembered that these advantages are not always essential to have and other materials which lack them often make up for this in their pleasing appearance. It is largely a matter of choosing the right material for the purpose. For example the area adjacent to the fuel store and the place where dustbins are kept will be well served by being cast *in situ* concrete paving. The path through the rhododendrons to the garden bench would probably look better paved with bricks.

The base. Most paths and paved areas are better for being constructed on a sound base of hardcore (fig. 31). First the ground

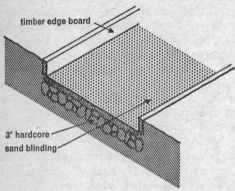

Fig. 31. A base for a garden path

should be cleared of vegetation and topsoil and, if necessary, levelled. The hardcore, comprising clean broken bricks or stones, should be compacted to a level of 3 ins. It should be 'blinded', or covered over, with a layer of sand or ashes. Alternatively cinders may be used instead of hardcore.

Concrete

A suitable mix for concrete paving is one part of cement to two parts of sand and three parts of coarse aggregate. Alternatively a mix composed of one part of cement to four parts of all-in aggregate is satisfactory. It is important to use the right mix, and materials should be measured carefully. Builders use gauge boxes made of wood or metal, but a set of clean buckets will serve the purpose.

The area to be paved should be cleared of vegetation and topsoil and levelled. Timber edge boards should then be fitted. Paths should be marked out in bays 4 ft to 5 ft long. Sufficient concrete for one bay should be mixed at a time.

If the concrete is to be hand mixed, the sand and aggregate should be measured out and mixed together first. The cement is then added and thoroughly mixed in. Form a crater in the mixed material and add the water. The amount of water will depend on the aggregate. A 'wet' mix should be avoided at all costs as this results in weak concrete.

Before laying the concrete the ground should be wetted (but not flooded). The concrete is then spread in position. A board slightly longer than the width of the path should be used to work the concrete into place, first with a chopping action and then with a sawing action. The finished effect of tamping in this method makes a suitably non-slip surface, but there are other finishes which give an interesting appearance and are equally serviceable. For instance the aggregate can be exposed by brushing the surface shortly after laying.

Once the paving has been laid and its surface finished it should be kept moist for several days whilst it is drying out. The best way to do this is to place sacks on top which are kept damp. Concrete which dries out too quickly will not attain its full strength. Paths and paving should be laid with a slight camber or fall to ensure that water does not lie in puddles. Paving against the house should, of course, drain to the far edge or into a gully.

Precast concrete paving slabs

Precast concrete paving slabs are commercially available in a variety of sizes, colours, and finishes. Names and addresses of suppliers are available from the Building Centres.

The area to be paved should be prepared as described for *in situ* concrete except that edge boards are not necessary. The edges should be marked with lines of string stretched over wooden pegs driven into the ground.

Slabs may be laid dry simply by bedding them on a well-compacted layer of sand or fine ashes 1 in. deep. If it is desired to avoid the inevitable settling of the slabs they should be bedded in mortar. A suitable mix for the mortar is 1 part cement to 3 parts sand. It should be spread evenly to a depth of about 1 in. and the slabs bedded one at a time and tapped lightly into position with the handle of the trowel. The slabs can be butted up against one another or a joint left between them which is subsequently grouted with mortar.

Stone paving

Certain natural stones are suitable for paving. They include the sandstones, the coarser limestones, and granite. York stone is commonly used for this purpose. It should be laid as described above on sand or fine ashes or on a mortar bed.

Brick paving

Most hard, well-burnt bricks are suitable for the purpose. A well-fired London stock, for example, would serve very well, though common stocks, which tend to be under-fired, will break down under exposure.

The normal method of laying on the prepared base described above is on a bed of sand or of lime and sand to the proportions of 1:4. Joints should be grouted. The width of joint will depend on the brick. For example engineering bricks which have a precise outline can be laid with $\frac{1}{8}$-in. wide joints, whereas less even bricks, such as stocks, should have as much as $\frac{3}{8}$ in.

Granite setts

This is a traditional material with a very hard-wearing surface. Setts are laid on the prepared base on a 1-in. bed of sand. They should be well rammed. It is usual to fill the joints ($\frac{3}{8}$ in. wide) with chippings before running in the grout.

Cobbles

This material makes a most attractive pavement, though, of course, it is not suited to wheeled traffic. Cobbles come from beaches and river beds, though it is illegal for you to help yourself to your own supply. Cobbles may be purchased from firms who have rights over certain beaches.

The normal method of laying is to place 2 ins. of sand over the prepared base. A 2 in. thickness of concrete (1:2:4 mix with small aggregate) is next placed on the sand and the cobbles pressed into this concrete by hand until they protrude by the desired amount.

Defects and remedies

Floorboards. Loose, squeaking floorboards are both a nuisance and a potential cause of accidents. They should be re-nailed as soon as they become loose. If a damaged floorboard has to be replaced, a method of removing it is to drill a number of holes across the board with a brace and large bit and join these up with a chisel and

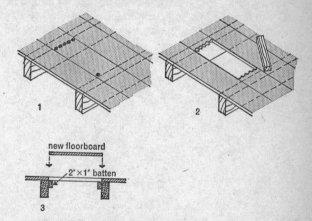

Fig. 32. Replacing a defective floorboard
1 Drill holes through the defective board alongside the joists
2 Link up the holes by cutting through with a chisel and mallet; remove the defective section of board
3 Nail short lengths of 2 in. × 1 in. batten to the sides of the joists; drop new length of floorboard into position and nail to battens

mallet. The board can then be prised up. Since the new length of board must be supported on the joists, the defective board should be cut out as close to the joists as possible (fig. 32) and the short piece of board between the cut and the centre of the joist subsequently removed with chisel and mallet. Alternatively a short length of 2-ins. × 1-in. timber can be screwed to the side of the joist, flush with the top, and the new length of floorboard nailed to this.

Floor tiles. Broken or cracked clay or quarry tiles should be removed with a cold chisel and hammer and the bedding also hacked out.

Concrete paving. Hollows and cracks often form in concrete paths due to settlement. Levelling of the area concerned with a thin screed feathered out at the edges is seldom satisfactory.

The most effective way to repair the concrete is to hack out the defective area with a cold chisel to a depth of at least 1 in. The new concrete will then be of a sufficient uniform depth to withstand wear. Broken edges of paving also should be hacked back to a clean line. A form board secured to pegs driven into the ground must then be placed in position before the new concrete is poured.

CHAPTER 6

Internal walls and ceilings

The internal walls of a house, sometimes referred to as *partitions*, may or may not be load-bearing. If they help to support the weight of floors and roof they are load-bearing. If they support only their own weight they are non load-bearing. Should structural alterations be contemplated, involving the removal of a wall or the cutting of a large opening, it is important to find out first whether the wall is load-bearing: if it is, means of supporting its load will have to be provided beforehand. In these circumstances an architect or a builder should be consulted.

Construction of internal walls

The construction of internal walls usually takes one of the following forms.

Brick. Brick walls are normally $4\frac{1}{2}$ ins. thick (width of one brick) plus the thickness of plaster on both sides, making a total thickness of about 6 ins. In older houses internal walls may be 9 ins. thick (two bricks wide) plus the thickness of plaster, making a total of about $10\frac{1}{2}$ ins.

Block. Walls constructed of blocks may be 2, 3, or 4 ins. thick plus thickness of plaster. There are many types of blocks, falling into two main groups: those made of clay and those made of concrete. Many are hollow, the main reason being to reduce weight, and types are available into which it is easy to drive a nail to hang a picture or fix shelves.

Concrete blocks used for house building are classified according to their composition or, more exactly, the nature of the aggregate with which the cement is mixed. Aggregates include clinker, foamed slag, exfoliated vermiculite, and expanded substances, such as clay. There are also aerated concrete blocks and blocks made of 'no fines' concrete, a form of concrete which does not include sand in its composition.

Building blocks are relatively light in weight and many have good thermal insulation properties. Hence it is common these days to use them for the inner leaf of cavity walls. Most blocks are much larger than a standard house brick, some being as much as 18 ins. long by 9 ins. high, but different types vary in size.

Timber framing. When lath and plaster was the conventional method of finishing walls and ceilings, internal walls were constructed with a timber frame. Although timber lath and plaster is rarely used in modern building, timber framed construction is still employed, but the usual method of finishing a wall is to surface it with a wallboard, such as plasterboard, nailed to the timber framing.

Finishes

The surfaces of a brick or block wall are almost always plastered. At one time it was usual for this plaster to be composed of lime and sand. This type of plaster is soft. Today plasters are generally of gypsum which provides a harder, denser surface than lime. Plaster is normally applied in two coats to a total thickness of about $\frac{3}{4}$ in.

In lath and plaster construction, softwood laths, about 1 in. wide by $\frac{3}{16}$ in. thick and spaced about $\frac{1}{4}$ in. apart, are nailed to the timber framing. This provides the 'key' to which the plaster is applied.

There are many types of building boards used for lining or finishing walls and ceilings. The most common is plasterboard, $\frac{3}{8}$ in. thick, to which a thin coat of plaster, called a 'skim' coat, is applied to provide a smooth jointless finish.

Plasterboard is often used to provide a finish to brick or block walls. This method of construction, known as *dry lining*, is described in chapter 3.

Fixing into internal walls

If you want to hang a picture or fit some shelves it is necessary to make a fixing into the wall. The ease with which this can be done depends on the construction of the wall. If it is timber framed with, say, a lath and plaster finish, it is sometimes possible to locate the studs (timber uprights) by probing with a bradawl, then nailing or screwing through the plaster into a stud. Some types of brick and block can be nailed into. Builders' merchants and ironmongers sell special nails for the purpose.

When brickwork is too hard or, at the other extreme, too soft for direct nailing or screwing, it will be necessary to *plug* the wall. The conventional way of doing this is with timber plugs which are small pieces of hardwood forced into pre-drilled holes in the wall. These days it is more usual to use one of the many proprietary wall plugs on the market, such as Rawlplug.

Never attempt to fix only into the plaster. In old houses especially this is often soft and quite unable to support anything but the lightest loads.

Rawlplug. The method of fixing with a Rawlplug is as follows. First make a hole with a cold chisel or a hand or electric drill using a masonry bit, then clean it out by blowing into it. The hole should be only large enough in diameter to be able just to force the Rawlplug in. Next turn the screw one or two times into the Rawlplug and guide the Rawlplug into the hole by means of the screw. When it has been pushed right in, turn the screw in the plug until the shank is about to enter. Withdraw the screw, fit the bracket or fitting in position, insert the screw into the plug again, and screw up until tight.

If the brickwork and plaster is soft and it is impossible to avoid forming a hole larger than intended, a plug can be made with the use of one of the proprietary plastic materials now on the market. These usually consist of asbestos fibres impregnated with cement which must be immersed in water before use in order to produce a pliable compound. This is then rammed into the hole and packed tight. The screw hole should be started by piercing the plastic with a nail or bradawl.

In a hollow block or timber-framed wall, direct fixing by nail or plugging and screwing may not be practicable. In this case one of the patent devices for fixing into wallboards or hollow partitions should be used such as a spring toggle bolt, described overleaf.

Spring toggle. First drill a hole through the wallboard or face of the hollow block through which both parts of the toggle, when pressed together, can be pushed. Having inserted the toggle, screw the head so that the two parts of the toggle are drawn tight against the inside face of the wallboard or block.

Plaster repairs

Like most building trades, plastering is a skilled job and one which the average amateur should not expect to undertake unless he has an aptitude and considerable enthusiasm. However, repairing or patching plaster in small areas is a task which most householders should be prepared to attempt. Small holes can be patched and cracks filled with a proprietary filler applied with a filling knife (see chapter 14). For larger patches it will be necessary to mix a batch of plaster and apply it with a trowel. Certain basic tools are required, as follows. A steel trowel, a hawk for holding a small quantity of plaster from which it is removed by the trowel and applied to the wall (this tool is in the form of a 12-in. square of timber with a round handle underneath, about 4 ins. long and $1\frac{1}{2}$ ins. diameter: it can be made by the handyman), a setting brush for applying water to the wall (an old distemper brush will do), a mixing board which is simply a flat, clean surface on which the ingredients for the plaster are mixed (this can be made out of tongued and grooved flooring boards fixed to a couple of 3-in. $\times$ $1\frac{1}{2}$-in. battens at the back: it should be about 3 ft square), and finally a couple of stout, clean buckets.

Preparing the surface. All the old, drummy plaster must be hacked off, using a cold chisel and bricklayer's hammer if necessary, and the bare brickwork exposed. The surface should then be brushed down with a wire brush to remove all loose particles. Finally the wall should be thoroughly wetted by throwing water on to it with the setting brush. It is then ready for the plaster.

Mixing the plaster. Plaster should be mixed on the mixing board, the surface of which should have been thoroughly cleaned immediately after its last use. Use a proprietary make of gypsum plaster and follow the manufacturer's instructions carefully. Make sure that the sand is clean: do not use beach sand as it contains salt which can cause efflorescence in the finished work. Plaster and sand should be mixed together before any water is added. The mix should be used at once.

Applying the plaster. There are a few simple rules to be observed. Firstly, when taking plaster off the hawk remember to move the hawk with the trowel in the direction of the wall or surface being worked on. Push the plaster on to the wall, using a fair degree of pressure, and gradually flatten the trowel towards the surface as the plaster is spread. Keep the trowel slightly on edge so that it is not quite in the same plane as the wall. If it is tilted too much it will scrape rather than spread the plaster and is likely to result in a series of wavy lines. If it is too flat it will tend to stick to the plaster by suction. If the thickness of old plaster which the patch must match is not too great it may be possible to carry out the repair with one coat of plaster. If not, two coats must be applied. The finishing coat should be quite thin and applied as soon as the first coat has set. Keep the surface of the trowel wet.

Ceilings

When floors and roofs are of timber construction the ground-floor ceiling and the upper-floor ceiling are fixed to the upper-floor joists and the ceiling joists respectively. Ceilings are usually of plasterboard, sometimes fibreboard. The former may be painted or papered direct, though it is normal to finish the surface with a single skim coat of plaster and sometimes with two coats. Fibreboard is generally decorated direct.

At one time ceilings were commonly constructed of lath and plaster: wood laths, about 1 in. × $\frac{3}{16}$ in. thick, were nailed to the joists about $\frac{1}{4}$ in. apart and thus formed a key for the plaster. These days metal laths are used instead of wood. One of the most popular forms of metal lath is expanded metal lathing, which is sheet steel so cut that it can be expanded, that is stretched, to form a diamond mesh. It is fixed to the underside of joists and the sharp edges of the mesh form an effective key for plaster.

Floors and roofs constructed of concrete generally have the

T – D

plaster ceiling finish trowelled direct on to the underside of the concrete.

Defects and remedies

Rising damp. This occurs in walls when there is no dampcourse or when the dampcourse has become defective. Methods of treatment recommended in chapter 3 for external walls are not all advisable for internal walls. For example applying a waterproof render is not necessarily satisfactory because, if applied to both sides of the wall, the effect will be to seal the wall and force the damp to rise further up the wall. One of the most permanent treatments, short of inserting a dampcourse, is to apply a dry lining as described in chapter 3.

Roof leaks. Roof leaks due to a broken slate or tile cause damp walls and upper-floor ceilings. Water entering in this way does not necessarily come through the ceiling immediately below the leak for it may run along a rafter before dropping off on to the ceiling.

Defects to the roof covering and methods of treatment are described in chapter 2.

Leaking pipes. Damp patches on walls and ceilings may be the result of a pipe leaking somewhere, a blocked gutter or downpipe or a defective joint in a water pipe for example. Another cause is water penetration through a parapet. This is likely to occur as the result of faulty constructional design or a defective dampcourse. The subject is discussed in chapter 3.

Condensation. Condensation is a cause of damp walls and ceilings. In flat roof construction in which the ceiling is attached direct to the underside of the roof structure, condensation on the surface of the top-floor ceiling is a common problem. The cause of condensation and the conditions necessary to avoid it are discussed in chapter 3. In good modern construction, condensation is avoided so far as ceilings are concerned either by providing a *vapour barrier* or adequate insulation. A vapour barrier often consists of a sheet of reinforced felt laid underneath the insulation to prevent moisture-laden air reaching the cold face. Another method is to use aluminium foil-backed plasterboard for the ceiling. If serious condensation of the top-floor ceiling occurs it may be advisable to obtain expert advice from an architect.

Cracks: shrinkage during drying out. A certain amount of shrinkage is likely to occur in all new buildings during the period when they are drying out. The result is fine cracks in the surface of the plaster. These cracks are not serious, though they may be unsightly. Cracks in plaster may also be caused by vibration such as heavy or violent movement on upper floors of the house. If they are carefully filled with a proprietary filler immediately prior to redecoration they should not reappear. Cracks which persistently reappear may be caused either by foundation movement or by movement due to thermal expansion and contraction. Foundation movement is not necessarily serious but professional advice should be sought if evidence of associated cracking appears elsewhere such as in partitions and external walls.

Foundation movement. It is always possible that persistent cracks may be the result of foundation movement as described in chapter 3. Under-pinning of the foundations may be necessary. In any case expert advice should be sought from an architect.

Deflection of joists. One cause of cracks in ceilings, apart from shrinkage, is deflection of the ceiling joists. This generally occurs when the joists are not sufficiently robust or are not adequately stiffened. This does not necessarily mean that the ceiling is in a dangerous condition and likely to fall down. On the contrary all joists and beams are designed to undergo a certain amount of deflection within a permissible limit. Even this limit is well within a margin of safety. None the less deflection can result in cracking of the plaster. If this appears to be the cause of cracks expert advice should be sought on means of strengthening the ceiling supports.

Plaster defects. In new work, patches of loose plaster or pitting of the surface is due to faulty materials and/or workmanship. In very old houses loose patches are generally due to the plaster having perished. Treatment must depend on which of these conditions applies and the extent of the defect.

In new work, loose plaster should be cut out and the area patched. The defect should not then recur. If pitting, popping, or blowing of the plaster has occurred the holes can be filled in the usual way before redecoration, using a proprietary filler applied with a filling knife. But there is no guarantee that the same trouble will not recur. It may be advisable, if the pitting is extensive and unsightly, to apply lining paper before redecoration or alternatively to paper the walls or ceiling.

In old houses where loose plaster is extensive the only effective cure may be to hack off the plaster and re-plaster or, in the case of walls, apply a dry lining. If walls are of lath and plaster the best solution, if rather drastic, is to remove the whole of the plaster and laths and start anew using plasterboard or fibreboard fixed to the existing timber framing. If the studs in the timber framing behind the lath and plaster can be located and the condition of the plaster is not too bad, plasterboard or fibreboard can be fixed over it, nailed through into the studs.

In the case of ceilings also, particularly if their general condition is poor, the most effective remedy is to replace the old lath and plaster with plasterboard or fibreboard. All the laths and old plaster must be stripped off and the new plasterboard or fibreboard nailed direct to the ceiling joists. It may be necessary to fit noggings (short pieces of timber) between the joists to provide adequate support for the ceiling board. If the condition of the old ceiling is not too bad and the ceiling joists can be located, it may be possible to fix the new ceiling through the old into the joists.

Stains and discoloration. Dirt from the air tends to collect on all surfaces and the rate at which it does so increases with the difference in temperature between a cool surface and warm air. Since the resistance to the flow of heat through a material varies with the material, it follows that in composite construction (construction using materials of differing resistance to heat flow) some parts of the construction will be colder than others. They constitute 'cold bridges'. The amount of dirt deposited on the surface of the construction varies according to the size and location of the cold bridges and the effect is described as *pattern staining*. As an example, in lath and plaster ceiling construction the wood laths offer higher resistance to the passage of heat than does the plaster between the laths. The latter thus forms cold bridges and pattern staining occurs. In this case the remedy would normally be to provide thermal insulation above the ceiling. See chapter 10.

CHAPTER 7

Cold water system

How the system works

The cold water supply to a house comes from the water authority's main in the street. The main is buried underground as is the supply pipe coming from it to the house. Pipes buried deep enough in the ground do not freeze up in cold weather.

A typical layout for the water supply is illustrated in fig. 33. The supply is carried from below ground level to a storage tank (the *cistern*) in the roof space. From the cistern, branch pipes supply all the fittings.

From the point where it enters the house to the point where it discharges into the cistern it is called the service pipe (popularly referred to as the rising main) and the pressure in the pipe is subject to the pressure from the water authority's main. It is usual to take a branch pipe direct from the rising main to the kitchen sink so that the kitchen tap can be used for drinking water.

Normally cold water pipes are made of lead, lead alloy, steel, wrought iron, or copper. In recent years, however, considerable development has taken place in the use of polythene, a form of plastic. In a modern house the pipes may be of this material.

CISTERN

A cistern is merely a tank for storing the household water supply and is normally mounted on a platform in the roof space. It is fed by the service pipe discharging into it through a ball valve. At one time cisterns were made of sheet lead and, in very old houses, lead cisterns are still in use. These days most cisterns are constructed of galvanized mild steel, although asbestos cement is also used.

The capacity of a cistern depends upon the size of the household. Water authorities vary in their requirements. The Model Building By-laws stipulate a minimum storage capacity of 25 gallons when only cold taps are served and 50 gallons when both hot and cold are supplied. The minimum requirements of the Metropolitan Water Board are 50 and 80 gallons respectively.

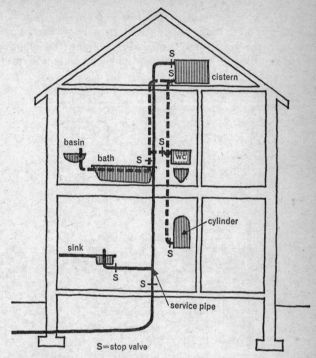

Fig. 33. Typical layout for cold water supply

BALL VALVE

This is a device for controlling the flow of water into the cistern from the rising main. It comprises a spherical float, made of copper or plastic, which rests on the surface of the water in the cistern, and a lever arm which is pivoted at the other end. The pivoted end controls a piston fitted with a rubber washer and is attached to the rising main. When water is drawn off through one of the taps in the house, its level in the cistern drops and the float drops with it. As it drops it releases the piston, opens the end of the rising main, and water flows in to refill the cistern. When it reaches a pre-determined level the rising float cuts off the water from the rising main.

The purpose of the overflow pipe from a cistern is to warn you when the level of the water in the cistern is rising above the normal line at which the ball valve shuts off the supply. When this happens it means that the ball valve is not functioning properly. This may

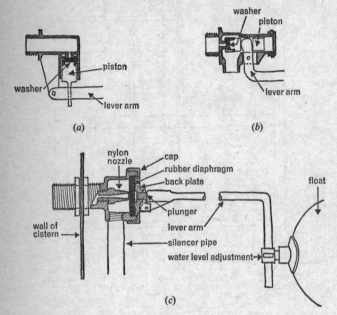

Fig. 34. Types of ball valve (*a*) Croydon; (*b*) Portsmouth; (*c*) Garston

be because: (i) the washer at the piston has become defective; (ii) the float is perforated and has water in it; (iii) a deposit of grit or lime has formed. The defects and remedies are discussed on page 107.

The two main types of ball valve are the 'Croydon' (fig. 34a) and the 'Portsmouth' (fig. 34b). The Building Research Station, after a period of experimentation, has produced a design called the 'Garston' ball valve (fig. 34c). It has been on the market for some years now and is made by several manufacturers and sold under different trade names.* It was designed to overcome three disadvantages found in other types of valve: (i) early damage to the seating; (ii) sticking of the piston; (iii) excessive noise. Its chief features are a nylon nozzle and a rubber diaphragm which stops the flow of water when it is pressed against the nozzle by the plunger. The diaphragm keeps the moving parts of the valve dry and hence free from corrosion. Movement of the plunger is controlled by the usual float on a lever arm. The float end of the lever arm, however, is bent down and the float clamped to it by a thumb screw. The required water level in the cistern can be adjusted according to the height on the bent-down section of lever arm at which the float is clamped.

STOP VALVE

Everybody knows what a tap is. In the plumbing trade it is sometimes called a 'cock' or a 'valve'. A stop valve, therefore, is merely a type of tap, one which is fitted to a pipe to shut off the flow of water through the pipe. Technically its correct name is isolating valve.

In domestic cold water systems the regulations require that a stop valve be placed on the service pipe immediately after it enters the house. Other stop valves are usually fitted in the following positions: (1) near the kitchen sink; (2) just before the storage cistern; (3) just before the w.c. cistern (it is desirable to have a stop valve on the outlet side of the cistern also). Normally these stop valves are left turned on, but in the event of a burst pipe or some other accident or when replacing a washer in a tap, the nearest stop valves should be turned off, thus isolating that section of pipe.

Some water authorities require an additional stop valve just outside the boundary to which they have sole access.

Frost protection

No part of the house is more susceptible to frost damage than the plumbing. Freeze-ups and burst pipes may be caused by:

* The B.R.S. does not, of course, manufacture the 'Garston' or any other ball valve. It is purely a research organization.

(1) An unheated house in which the air temperature (around pipes) drops below freezing point.

(2) Incorrect pipe layout.

(3) Unlagged or inadequately lagged pipes.

Remember that pipes cannot burst if there is no water in them to freeze up. If you are likely to leave the house empty (and therefore unheated) during the cold weather, turn off the water at the main stop valve and turn on all taps until they run dry.

Prepare for the winter in the following way:

(1) Find out where the main stop valve is and make sure that it can be turned off easily and tightly.

(2) Familiarize yourself with the layout of all piping.

(3) Replace the washers in all dripping taps. This is a service which some water authorities will carry out for you if necessary.

Should a pipe freeze up, the simplest way to unfreeze it is to apply rags soaked in hot water. But first check that there are no cracks or splits in the pipe. Burst pipes cause flooding, not when they freeze up but when there is a thaw. Use several pieces of rag applied in turn. Time and patience will thaw out the pipe: it is inadvisable to use a blowlamp to do this. As soon as it is thawed, buy some pipe lagging and securely lag the pipe. This is insurance against the same thing happening again.

Should the rising main burst, turn off the stop valve immediately. Should any other pipe burst, turn off the stop valve on it or, if there isn't one, turn off the stop valve on the rising main and open all taps.

There is no doubt that intelligent layout of piping can help considerably to eliminate freezing. Whilst it is the responsibility of the architect and the builder to achieve this in the first place, some vulnerable positions may have been overlooked. A case in point is when the service pipe (rising main) is carried up the inside face of an external wall. It is very likely to freeze up at the point where it passes through the ceiling and is exposed to draughts through the eaves. This is often an impossible position to get at to lag the pipes.

Lagging. Pipes in the roof space should be lagged, particularly if there is insulation above the top-floor ceiling. So should pipes in any other positions likely to be affected by frost. The lagging of pipes is something which the householder should be able to do himself. Builders' merchants stock many types of strip insulating materials which are wrapped spirally around the pipes and secured in place with wire or stout string. Rigid moulded sections of mineral wool or glass wool are also available for the purpose.

Storage cisterns should be lagged, but do *not* lag the underside of the cistern. This is particularly important when there is ceiling insulation, as no warmth from below would get to the tank at all. Cistern insulating casings can be obtained from builders' merchants. These usually take the form of compressed straw or foamed polystyrene slabs with holes pre-cut for the various pipes. They are normally held in position by binding wire around the cistern. The lid is a slab which is simply laid on top.

An alternative is to construct two boxes, one fitting over the other. These are fitted around the cistern and the space between the two boxes filled with loose insulating material such as rock wool or exfoliated vermiculite.

Defects and remedies

BALL VALVE

Defective washer. The procedure for replacing a defective washer is as follows. Turn off the stop valve just before the cistern. Remove the cover of the cistern. Using a pair of pliers, withdraw the split pin which holds the lever arm in place and this will then come away. If you have a 'Portsmouth' type ball valve it will be necessary to unscrew the cap on the end of the piston chamber. The piston should then be prised out with a screwdriver, the old washer removed, and a new one inserted.

Perforated float. Turn off the stop valve as above. Remove the float from the lever arm. If you then shake it you will be able to hear if there is water inside, in which case it is advisable to replace it with a new plastic ball valve. Do not forget to turn the stop valve on again after reassembly. When repairing a w.c. cistern it should be flushed after the stop valve has been turned off just prior to taking the ball valve to pieces.

Grit or lime deposit. This is a problem which occurs in hard water districts. The effect of corrosion and lime deposit on the piston and the valve body can cause the piston to stick in the open position. The valve should be dismantled and cleaned periodically and the piston greased. In newly built houses similar trouble may occur because of grit, if the water system has not been flushed after installation as it should be.

A less common defect is for the valve to stick in the closed position, thus cutting off the water supply. In houses which have been unoccupied for some time this often occurs because dirt and lime have dried out on the working parts. The remedy is to work the lever arm up and down a few times. If this does not cure the trouble it will be necessary to dismantle the valve and clean it thoroughly.

TAPS

Leak around spindle. There are two places where taps commonly leak. One of these is around the spindle. The cause may be merely that the gland nut is loose and needs tightening with a spanner. If, however, tightening fails to stop the leak, the trouble almost certainly is likely to be inadequate packing in the stuffing box. If the tap has a cover this must be removed. To do so it is often necessary first to remove the handle of the tap, usually held in position by a set screw. Take care when removing the cover as it can easily be disfigured. Some covers have a nut at the bottom and can be undone easily with a large adjustable spanner. Wrap some rag around the cover before applying the spanner. Unscrew the spindle nut and pick out the packing in the stuffing box with a piece of wire. Wind some soft string around the spindle and replace the nut. It is not usually necessary to cut off the water supply to do this job.

Defective washer. The other place where leaks occur is at the outlet. This is due to a defective washer.

Apart from wasting water, a dripping tap can be a source of irritation. Replacing a washer is a fairly simple operation (fig. 35). The nearest stop valve should be turned off to cut off the supply to the tap. Turn the tap on until it runs dry. Remove the handle of the tap which is usually held in position by a set screw. If there is a cover unscrew this and remove it. The nut on the upper part of the tap should then be unscrewed with a spanner and pulled out. At the bottom end of this assembly is the plunger to which the washer is attached. Unscrew the little nut holding it in position, prise off the old washer, fit the new, and reassemble.

Taps are now made which can be re-washered without turning off the water. One make, a 'Supatap', is illustrated in fig. 35.

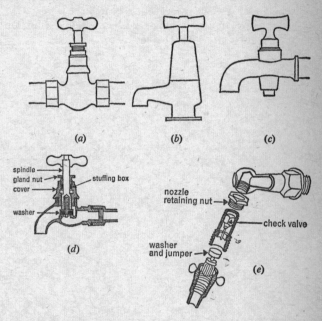

Fig. 35. Types of tap (*a*) stop valve; (*b*) pillar cock; (*c*) plug cock; (*d*) bib cock; (*e*) Supatap

Spare washers can be bought from an ironmonger or a builders' merchant. Washers are made for hot and cold taps and for ball valves, and when buying one it is as well to mention the type of tap or ball valve in which it is to be fixed. If in doubt, remove the old washer and take that along when purchasing a new one.

Noise in the plumbing system. Water hammer is the clanging or knocking noise which occurs when a tap is turned off. It is usually brought about by the action of plug cocks or automatic (self-closing) taps. It often occurs where there are long runs of pipe. Occasionally it is caused by a defective ball valve. The remedy is to replace the fittings with screw-down bib cocks or efficient ball valves as the case may be. Plumbers' advice may be necessary.

Excessive noise often results from ill-fitting or worn washers on taps. The obvious cure is to replace the washer. Check that the gland is not loose, in which case it should be tightened.

Other sources of noise, including noisy w.c.s and vibration noise in pipes, are dealt with in chapter 10.

CHAPTER 8

Hot water system

Hot water requirements

Family requirements for hot water vary not only according to the size of the family but also according to the family's habits. The number of fittings in a house also affect the total amount of hot water used. It is perhaps not surprising that the more fittings there are in a house the greater the inducement to use hot water. In designing a system the 'peak' demand period is taken as the hot water required during the busiest time of the day, say, early morning. It is customary to provide a storage cylinder capable of storing enough hot water for not less than an hour and a half's requirements and a boiler capable of heating this quantity in this time. It is not uncommon to provide $2\frac{1}{2}$ to 3 hours storage. Average hot water consumption of various fittings is usually taken as:

bath	25 gallons
shower	5 to 8 gallons
basin	2 gallons
sink	3 to 5 gallons

Experience shows that the temperature at which this hot water is required at draw off point is usually:

bath	100–110° F
shower	95–100° F
basin	100–110° F
sink	110–140° F*

These temperatures are achieved by mixing hot water with cold: the temperature of the water in the storage cylinder needs to be considerably higher.

* and higher for washing up.

Forms of water heating

Domestic hot water installations are generally of two kinds; either they store hot water, for drawing off when required, or they supply it 'instantaneously'. Storage systems provide large quantities of hot water fairly quickly and any family whose requirements are large should use a system of this type. An instantaneous heater is more suitable for a small household of 2 to 3 people. It supplies hot water instantaneously, but at a lower rate of flow than does a storage system.

There are several forms of storage hot water systems, principally the type in which water is heated in a boiler, solid fuel, oil- or gas-fired, and stored in a cylinder, or the type in which hot water is stored in a gas-fired or electric storage heater. Instantaneous (non-storage) systems take the form of a gas heater which may serve a number of fittings, such as sink, basin, and bath, or only one fitting.

Boiler system

The independent boiler and the back boiler operate as circulating systems (fig. 36). Cold water is supplied to the base of the storage cylinder from a cistern, usually mounted in the roof space, and then passes to the boiler where it is heated. The hot water returns to the cylinder so that water is circulating between the two. The service to the various taps over fittings also leads off from the cylinder. This system of gravity circulation can also be used in conjunction with partial or full central heating by circulating water around the house to radiators or convectors in the various rooms. In this case the cylinder is an indirect type (see chapter 11).

It is always desirable to keep the length of draw-off pipes as short as possible, as well as the flow and return pipes. If there are a number of fittings to be served or if the distance to individual fittings is long, the system is often designed with a *secondary circulation* circuit. This runs from the cylinder (secondary flow), serves the various fittings, and returns to the cylinder (secondary return).

Pipes for hot water systems are usually either light gauge copper tube or galvanized wrought iron tube, as for cold water supply.

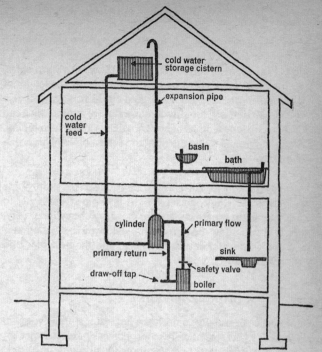

Fig. 36. Typical layout for hot water installation (gravity circulation)

Defects

This type of hot water system sometimes gives trouble, due almost always to faulty design or layout of the system. Common faults include:

Slow supply at taps. It is important that the size of pipe leading to each fitting is of the correct size, for example $\frac{1}{2}$ in. for a lavatory basin, $\frac{3}{4}$ in. for a bath. If the basin as well as the bath is supplied by a $\frac{3}{4}$-in. pipe, the result will be that water runs slowly at the taps as the flow is not adequate for the purpose. Sometimes slow delivery occurs when the pipe supplying the cylinder from the cistern is too small. Flow is also affected by the head of water (i.e. cold water cistern to taps) and by the length of draw-off pipes, which should be as short as possible.

Water not hot enough. Needless to say, water which is circulating in this way loses a certain amount of heat from the pipes. If the lengths of pipe between boiler and cylinder (flow and return pipes) are too long, excessive heat loss may occur. Ideally the length of flow and return pipes should not exceed 10–15 ft. Heat will also be lost if circulation is at too slow a rate, a state of affairs which can arise if there are long lengths of horizontal flow and return piping. It is always advisable to lag the flow and return pipes. This is discussed on page 106.

Water running hot then cold. This is usually due to the supply pipe to certain fittings being connected to the flow pipe from boiler to cylinder, whereas it should come from the top of the cylinder only. If water is drawn off at the taps from the flow pipe, circulation is affected and cold water enters the system and the flow pipe and may be drawn off at the taps.

Storage heaters

The storage heater usually comprises a hot water storage vessel in which there is a thermostatically controlled gas or electric heater. Both gas and electric types operate automatically, and the electric type and the smaller gas type do not need a flue.

Gas circulator. A gas circulator is a heater designed to be connected to the cylinder of a solid fuel circulating system so that it provides an alternative means of heating water during the summer. It can, however, also be used as the sole means of heating water throughout the year. The essential difference between a gas circulator and a gas storage heater is that the heating element is connected to the cylinder with circulating pipes in the case of the gas circulator, whereas in the storage heater it is integral with it.

Electric immersion heater. An electric immersion heater can be installed in the cylinder of a boiler circulating system to provide hot water during the summer.

Sink heaters. It will be seen from page 111 that hot water for the sink should be supplied at a higher temperature than is required for other fittings. Even when a full hot water system is installed in a house there is a good case for having a sink heater. Sink heaters are either electric or gas. The former is a storage vessel of $1\frac{1}{2}$, 2 or 3 gallons' capacity containing an immersion heater and controlled by thermostat. The latter may be a storage heater similar to the above or an instantaneous heater of which types can be obtained supplying hot water at three temperatures, warm (110° F), hot (140° F), and boiling.

Instantaneous heaters

Gas instantaneous heaters are either of the single-point or multi-point type. The single-point literally serves one fitting. Types are available for either the sink or the bath, the latter having an extended swivel spout, if required, to serve both bath and basin. The multi-point type will, of course, serve several fittings.

Conversion unit. This is a type of gas operated unit designed to be fitted in a back boiler fire to heat the water during summer or when the fire is out. It uses the same flue and ventilation as the fire and requires no additional pipes.

Lagging

Cold water pipes are lagged to prevent freeze-up in cold weather. It is equally important to lag hot water pipes, the reason in this case being to prevent heat loss. No hot water system can function at maximum efficiency and economy if heat lost through the pipes is excessive.

Insulating jackets are available for all standard sizes of cylinder. These are packed with mineral wool or glass wool. They should be fitted all around the cylinder and secured in position with wire or tape.

Pipes should be insulated as described in chapter 7. If draw-off lengths of pipe are not too long they need not be lagged, but the circulating pipes should always be lagged. It is worth lagging frequently used draw-off pipes such as the one serving the kitchen sink.

CHAPTER 9

Drains and waste plumbing

Most houseowners have only a hazy idea of the way the drainage system works. They are not particularly interested in the subject until something goes wrong with the drains. It is a tribute to the vigilance of local authority public health departments that faults seldom occur. This is not to say that the regulations governing drainage matters are as forward-looking as they might be. The purpose of these regulations is primarily to safeguard the health of the community, but they should not restrict the development of improved materials and techniques. Research organizations such as the Building Research Station are constantly looking into ways and means of improving the efficiency and reducing the cost of drainage installations.

The drainage system of a house can be divided broadly into two parts: that which is below ground (literally the drains) and that which is above, normally called the *waste and soil* plumbing.

Waste and soil pipes. Every sanitary fitting in a house is, or should be, connected to either a waste or a soil pipe. A w.c. is connected to a soil pipe. Other fittings, such as basin, bath, shower, kitchen sink, are connected to waste pipes. Until fairly recently drainage regulations required that waste pipes from fittings should pass immediately out of the house. The result is that most old houses (and, unfortunately, quite a few new ones) have their outside walls festooned with pipes. Today regulations permit waste pipes inside the house and, although it is more costly to install them there, it is much better to do so, for several reasons: frost attack is minimized, painting is less frequent, and the improvement to the appearance of the outside of the house is considerable.

The purpose of waste and soil pipes is to convey waste water and the discharge from w.c.s to the drains. In so doing, however, they must ensure that no foul air can get back from the drains through the fittings into the house. This is achieved by fitting a 'trap' to the waste pipe where it connects to the fitting. The trap always contains water and is thus an effective seal against the passage of air up the pipes. Of course every time a sink or a bath is emptied the water lying in the trap is displaced, but it is immediately replaced by the discharge from the fitting (in the case of the w.c. the flush from the cistern).

Soil pipes are different in that the trap is formed as part of the fitting (i.e. the w.c. pan).

Gully. When a waste pipe eventually goes underground it passes through a *gully* (fig. 37). This is merely another name for a type of trap and is usually made in salt glazed earthenware. A grating is

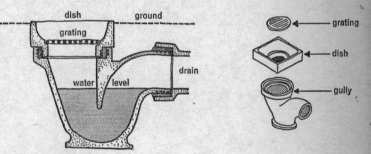

Fig. 37. Gully

fitted to the top at ground level to prevent leaves and garden rubbish falling into and blocking the trap.

It is advisable to clean out all gullies around the house every 12 months or so, especially the gully into which the sink waste discharges. Prise off the grating from the top of the gully and remove any rubbish which may have collected at the bottom. It is as well to scrub round the sides of the gully with an old scrubbing brush. When you have finished turn on the hot tap and run fresh hot water through it.

Manholes. The drains carry the waste and soil water to the sewer under the street. At each junction between a branch drain and the main drain and at each change of direction a manhole is situated.

This is a pit, built usually in brickwork, through which the drains pass as open channels. The manholes are big enough for a man to get into and pass a rod up the drain to clear it if it gets blocked. Manholes have covers over them at ground level, which are usually cast iron. It is as well to know the positions of all manholes in the drainage system and from time to time to lift the covers as they are liable to get jammed. One way to safeguard against this is to grease the grooves at the top of the manhole into which the manhole cover fits.

Ventilation. One of the basic principles of drainage design is to ensure that drains are adequately ventilated and the building by-laws require this. In most house installations this is normally done in one of two ways. The first method involves the provision of an *interceptor trap* (fig. 38) at a point just inside the house boundary.

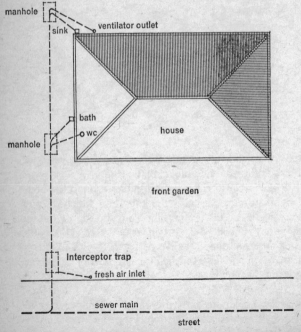

Fig. 38. Typical house drainage layout

This trap is housed in a chamber set in the ground so that it can be got at. The chamber has a low-level *fresh-air inlet* connected to it. At the top end of the system (i.e. a point beyond the furthermost fitting) is a high-level outlet. Quite often the upstairs w.c. is at the top end of the system and the soil pipe into which it discharges is merely extended up above the eaves to form the outlet ventilator. The top of this pipe should be fitted with a balloon of galvanized or copper wire to prevent birds nesting. Air which accumulates in a drain is warmer than the outside air and hence rises to the top end of the drainage system. Air currents moving across the exposed end of the outlet ventilator pull the air out of the drain and this is replaced by air entering the drain through the fresh air inlet.

The second method of ventilating drains does not involve the provision of an interceptor trap but relies on the ventilator at the top end of the house system for the discharge of foul air from the drains and fresh air inlets on the sewer. In this case both the house drains and the public sewer are, in effect, ventilated through the outlet ventilator.

Water closets. The contemporary w.c. has many antecedents most of which would be insanitary by present day standards and some of which still exist in very old houses. Today there are broadly two types of w.c. in use, normally constructed of white glazed fireclay or vitreous china formed in one piece with the pedestal and trap. The *washdown* type is still the most commonly used. The contents are removed when the trap overflows by gravity. The *siphonic* type is one in which the contents of the pan are emptied by siphonic action and not by the volume and velocity of water from the flushing cistern.

Defects and remedies

Blocked traps. If the w.c. trap becomes blocked it is advisable to call a plumber as he has special devices which can be poked down through the trap and he has other means of getting at the pipes. If a sink or basin waste becomes blocked, however, it is a relatively simple matter to free it. Place an empty bucket immediately underneath the nut at the base of the trap. Undo the nut with a wrench (anti-clockwise), being careful not to damage the thread or the trap may subsequently leak. The solid matter should then drop out if it has lodged at the base of the trap. Otherwise it may be necessary to poke about with a piece of stout wire or a screwdriver to clear the obstruction.

You should not wait until the sink waste blocks before performing this little operation. Because a certain amount of solid matter – small pieces of vegetable, tea leaves, etc. – invariably goes down the sink, it is advisable to remove the nut at the trap (don't forget the bucket) and scrape the trap clear, whenever the flow out of the sink through the trap appears restricted.

It is sometimes possible to free a blocked trap by applying a suction cup over the outlet. There should be about 1 in. of water in the bottom of the sink and the overflow should be covered up. The suction cup should be vigorously worked up and down. The sharp increase of pressure when forcing the cup down and the equally sharp suction effect of the upstroke often succeeds in dislodging an obstruction.

W.C. flushing cistern. There are not many faults which can occur in a w.c., other than blockage of the trap, described above. A badly chipped or cracked pan is a potential danger to health and it is well worth while replacing it with a new pan.

The w.c. flushing cistern is a more likely cause of trouble. The most common faults are (*a*) failure to flush when operated, and (*b*) excessive noise of water entering the cistern after flushing.

Failure to flush usually occurs because there is not enough water in the cistern. The ball valve is cutting off the supply before the cistern is filled. This can generally be overcome by bending the lever arm of the ball valve upwards. Do not bend it too far or water will come out of the overflow pipe.

Excessive noise during refilling of the cistern can be eliminated by fitting a silencer to the ball valve, provided, of course, that it is a type of ball valve to which this can be done. A silencer is simply a piece of pipe fitted to the outlet on the ball valve and extending nearly to the bottom of the cistern. The water refilling the cistern enters below water level. A considerably improved type of ball valve has been developed by the Building Research Station and is now marketed under the name the 'Garston' ball valve. This is described in chapter 7.

CHAPTER 10

Insulation, ventilation, and noise reduction

Insulation

The warmth in a house is gradually dissipated in the outside air. Heat is lost partly through the external walls, ground-floor, and roof, partly by the displacement of warmed air within by cold air from without. All building materials allow heat to pass through them to some extent. Those with the highest resistance to the passage of heat are generally termed *insulating* materials.

Much more is known these days about the thermal behaviour of building materials, and in the building of a house it is now possible to make considerable provision for keeping the heat in. By using materials in the structure itself which are themselves good insulators and by providing an insulating barrier against heat loss in such positions as the roof space above the top-floor ceiling and the space beneath the ground-floor, it will be possible to recover the cost many times over in the saving on fuel bills.

Much can be done to improve conditions in a house by providing thermal insulation at the most vulnerable points (fig. 39).

Ceiling

In a house with a pitched roof the space above the top-floor ceiling is not inhabited and does not require heating. Heat passing into it from the rooms below is therefore wasted. Provided there is an access hatch into the roof space, it is not a difficult task to lay insulation above the ceiling. Most builders' merchants stock insulating materials suitable for the purpose. These generally take the following forms:

Loose fill. This is usually rock wool, slag wool, mineral wool, glass wool, gypsum, exfoliated vermiculite, or granulated cork. It is supplied in bags. Pour it between the joists to a thickness of 2 ins., spreading it level, but do not compress it. Use a piece of timber cut as a template (fig. 40a). If possible, block off the ends of the joists at the eaves with pieces of wood fitted between the joists or strips

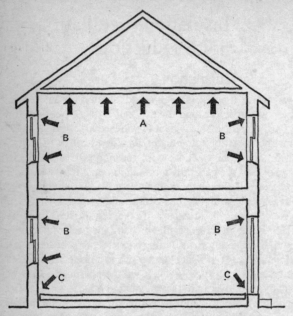

Fig. 39. Points of heat loss (A) through top floor ceiling; (B) around windows and door frames; (C) at skirtings

of building paper. Loose fill is particularly suitable if the space between joists varies or if there are obstructions or parts of the roof space which are difficult to get at.

Quilts. Insulating quilts of rock wool, slag wool, mineral wool, or glass wool are the most popular material for ceiling insulation. They are supplied in rolls in various lengths and widths for laying between the joists (fig. 40b). A thickness of 1in. is generally adequate depending on the type of insulating material. When ordering the quilt, give the width between the joists. Wider rolls may be obtained for laying across the tops of joists (fig. 40c). It is advisable to overlap the edges of rolls 3 ins. or so. Seal off the ends to prevent

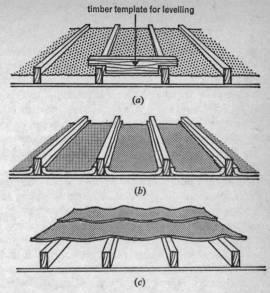

Fig. 40. Types of roof insulation (*a*) loose fill between the joists; (*b*) insulating quilts between the joists; (*c*) insulating quilts across the tops of joists

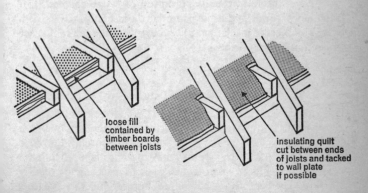

Fig. 41. Methods of sealing roof insulation at eaves

draughts (fig. 41). The quilt should be laid so that it sags between joists. Do not attempt to stretch it over the joists.

Aluminium foil. This is supplied in rolls 2 ft wide. The type which is backed with building paper should be laid over and tacked to the joists with the foil face downwards. It is important to prevent draughts getting into the space between joists, and sheets should be lapped about 3 ins. and sealed off at the ends of joists. There is another type which consists of two sheets of foil, one plain and one corrugated, stapled together. This may be laid either over the joists or between them. In either case the corrugations should be face downwards.

There are several points to bear in mind when putting down ceiling insulation. If using a type of quilt insulation, make sure the roll can be passed through the ceiling hatch. When moving about in the roof space take care to tread on the tops of ceiling joists, never between them, as the ceiling itself, whatever its construction, is not strong enough to take your weight. It is a good idea, before laying the insulation, to place some planks of wood across the joists so that you can move about without accidently treading between the joists and going through the ceiling. When laying a quilt across joists try to ensure that the insulation is turned down at the end of joists to prevent draughts coming through the eaves and blowing under the insulation. Do not insulate under the water cistern, but insulate around and on top of it (see chapter 7). If water pipes are not lagged make sure that the insulation covers them over. The effect of insulating the ceiling is to make the roof space a very much colder place.

Ground-floor

It is possible to insulate an existing suspended timber floor by taking up the floor boards and laying insulating quilts, aluminium foil, or fibreboard over the joists and then replacing the floor boards. As this will also involve removing and then refixing the skirtings, it would be easier and cheaper to place a good quality felt underlay beneath carpet or a bitumen underlay beneath linoleum.

External walls

A cavity brick wall has a much higher resistance to the passage of heat than a 9-in. thick solid brick wall, although both contain the same number of bricks. If the inner skin of the cavity wall is constructed in lightweight concrete blocks, the thermal resistance is further improved. In building a new house, adequate thermal resistance can be obtained by a careful choice of materials and construction. This is a matter on which your architect will advise you. Improving the thermal resistance of the walls of an existing house is not so simple. The usual technique is to nail softwood battens to the walls and fix plasterboard, which has an aluminium foil backing, to the battens. This technique is known as *dry lining* and is described in chapter 3. Perhaps some consolation can be found in the knowledge that, compared with other parts of the house, a comparatively small proportion of heat is lost through the walls.

Preventing draughts

Windows and doors. The most likely points are around windows and external doors. Several materials are available as 'draught stripping', ranging from felt or p.v.c. strip tacked or stuck in position to more complicated phosphor bronze sections (fig. 42). To prevent draughts blowing under doors, the most efficient draught excluder is the type which screws to the bottom of the door and lifts up and down with the action of the door. Most builders' merchants or ironmongers stock one or another of these materials and information and manufacturers' descriptive leaflets on insulating materials for ceilings, pipes, and cisterns and on draught stripping for windows and doors are available from the Building Centres (see appendix 2).

Floors. Draughts can blow through the cracks between boards. The best remedy is to lay carpet or linoleum or similar sheet or tile floor coverings (see chapter 5). One of the cheapest of these is hardboard, fixed with panel pins. A thickness of $\frac{1}{8}$ in. is usually adequate.

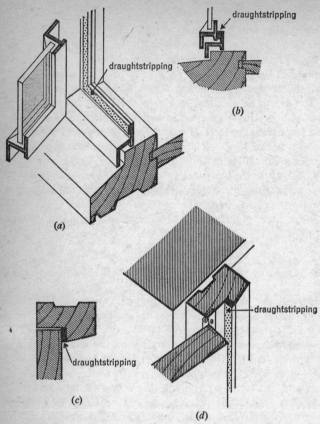

Fig. 42. The fitting of draughtstripping (*a*) and (*b*) metal window; (*c*) and (*d*) timber door

Skirtings. There is often a gap between the skirting and the floor through which draughts can blow. This gap can be sealed by nailing a timber quadrant or beading to the floor, hard up against the skirting (fig. 43).

Fireplaces. Open fires, solid fuel stoves, and fitted gas fires must have flues and require a certain amount of ventilation to function satisfactorily. Existing chimney flues, however, often cause excessive draughts. Solid fuel stoves and gas fires have a flue nozzle at the rear. If a sheet of metal or asbestos is fixed to the fireplace

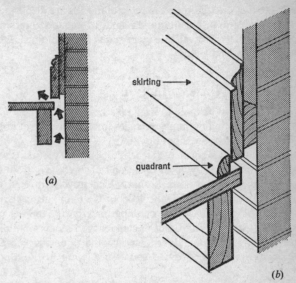

Fig. 43. Sealing skirtings from draught (*a*) passage of draught between floor and skirting; (*b*) quadrant fixed to floor against skirting

opening with a hole cut in it for the flue nozzle to pass through, draughts will be eliminated. For a gas fire, the hole should be slightly larger than the nozzle to ensure adequate ventilation.

Ventilation

While it is desirable to eliminate draughts, it is important not to seal up the house completely so that there is virtually no ventilation. Apart from ensuring regular air change for the sake of health, ventilation is necessary to prevent condensation, dry rot, and smoking chimneys.

Never block up air bricks which ventilate the space beneath a timber ground-floor as this will almost certainly lead to dry rot.

If the ventilation in a room does not appear to be adequate, it may be necessary to install an extractor fan. In a kitchen the presence of steam and cooking smells can be objectionable. To eliminate them it is necessary to accelerate the rate of air change, which is what an electrically operated fan will do. Such fans are usually fitted in the window. A number of models are displayed in the Design Centre in London and names of manufacturers and descriptive leaflets are available there and at The Building Centre, London (see appendix 2).

Noise reduction

Whereas much can be done to insulate a house against heat loss, there are not very many simple remedies for the nuisance of noise, whether coming from without or within.

Noise is either air-borne or 'structure-borne'. The first is self-evident: if you leave a window open, noise will come in from the street. Structure-borne noise is that which travels through the structure of the building (i.e. the walls or the floor) just as damp might do. The more massive a building material the more it will resist the passage of sound. But the tendency in modern building construction is towards lighter materials and thinner walls. The need to take steps to provide sound insulation is thus more important.

Do not confuse *sound transmission* with *sound absorption*. If you line the walls of a room with, say, fibreboard which is sound-absorbent, it will make the room quieter relative to the noises within it (e.g. the telephone or the radio), but it will not prevent the passage of sound through the walls from the next room.

Much can be done to reduce noise coming through the ceiling from the rooms above by a sensible choice of floor coverings. The worst problem is so-called 'impact' noise. Soft coverings in the form of thick fitted carpet or underfelt will go a long way towards minimizing this sort of noise.

If this does not reduce noise transmission to a tolerable level, it will probably be necessary to resort to a structural method of providing sound insulation. This may take the form of a layer of sand, slagwool, or similar material on top of the ceiling between the first-floor joists, a technique known as *pugging* (fig. 44), or it may involve forming a *floating floor* (fig. 45) or, again, it may mean

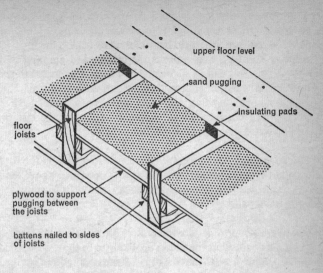

Fig. 44. Sound insulation by pugging

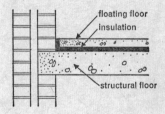

Fig. 45. A floating floor

using a combination of these techniques. If your noise problem is severe enough to suggest that any of these methods is required you should consult an architect to obtain expert advice.

Water closet. Apart from sound coming through the walls there are other sources of noise equally irritating. The noisy w.c. is a common problem. If you hear a rushing sound of water in the flush pipe when the chain is pulled, it is probably because the pipe is fitted hard against the wall and sound is transmitted from the pipe to the wall. One solution is to remove the clips holding the pipe to the wall and insert rubber or felt pads behind them.

Another form of w.c. noise is the hissing and gurgling of a filling cistern. This can be overcome by fitting a 'silencer' to the ball valve, provided, of course, that the ball valve is of a suitable type (see chapter 7, fig. 34). A silencer consists of a short length of pipe running from the ball valve to the bottom of the cistern. Incoming water then enters below the surface.

Storage tank. Noise which comes from a storage tank in the roof is usually the same hissing, gurgling noise described above, and can be remedied in the same way. It may also help to stand the tank on a felt pad.

Water pipes. Water pipes are themselves often the cause of noise. Unfortunately the worst offenders are likely to be those embedded in the wall. Pipes fixed to the face of a wall can be cured as described above by fitting felt or rubber pads behind the clips.

CHAPTER 11

Heating

Without doubt people are becoming more heating conscious and are prepared to spend more on heating their houses than they were before the war. Heating appliances and systems have been improved and developed enormously in this time. Financial assistance is available to those interested in installing full or partial central heating.

The subject of house heating is large enough to fill a book, and several books have been filled. This chapter is intended simply to describe the principles of house heating and to provide the householder with a working guide to the various forms of heating available to him at the present time. It emphasizes those systems suitable for installing in an existing house, although others, such as electric floor warming, are also discussed.

The householder is advised to seek expert guidance when considering a heating installation, particularly if a form of whole house heating is contemplated. For independent impartial advice, a heating and ventilating engineer or an architect should be consulted. Their respective professional institutions (see appendix 1) will provide names and addresses. Technical advice is also available from a number of organizations whose names and addresses are listed in appendix 2.

In 1956 the Clean Air Act became law. This empowers local authorities to declare Smoke Control Areas, in which it is an offence to emit smoke from a chimney. Within such areas it is necessary to use certain 'authorized fuels' and this must, of course, affect choice of heating system or appliance. In England and Wales authorized fuels are coke (all types), low volatile steam coals, anthracite, Phurnacite, Coalite, Rexco, gas, and electricity. Oil and coal are not authorized fuels, but may be used in equipment which is designed, maintained, and operated to produce no smoke: the onus is on the user.

The Coal Utilization Council, in association with the Solid Smokeless Fuels Federation, publishes a list of approved solid fuel appliances.* All appliances included in the list have been tested by the Domestic Solid Fuel Appliances Approval Council, an authority set up in 1959 and comprising representatives of the Ministry of Power, British Coking Industry Association, British Ironfounders' Association, National Coal Board, and The Gas Council. The C.U.C. points out that the absence of an appliance from the list does not necessarily mean that it is unsatisfactory. New models are continually being developed and many are not submitted for official test before appearing on the market. It goes without saying, however, that the claims of a manufacturer that his unlisted appliance is as good as, or better than, those recommended, or that it would certainly pass the tests, should be treated with reserve. The C.U.C. is prepared at any time to say whether a new appliance has been accepted for inclusion in the next edition of the list, but will not express any opinion on unlisted appliances.

The Gas Council issues a separate list for appliances burning all types of coke. It is called the 'Coke-burning Appliances Handbook'. The appliances listed have all been tested in one of the Gas Council laboratories. The Council also issues a list of approved domestic appliances which includes space heating, water heating, and refrigeration. Manufacturers of tested and approved appliances are entitled to attach the official Approval Seal. All Gas Boards and their authorized dealers have agreed to display and sell only those appliances which are on the approved list.

The British Electrical Development Association publishes a similar list for electrical appliances. Appliances included in the list have been tested at the Association's laboratories at Leatherhead in Surrey. In addition some Area Boards carry out tests and, as a rule, the Boards will only display and sell appliances tested and approved either by themselves or by the B.E.D.A.

In 1945 the Heating and Ventilating (Reconstruction) Committee of the Building Research Board of the Department of Scientific and Industrial Research, under the chairmanship of Sir Alfred Egerton, issued a report† which was a thorough investiga-

* Available from the C.U.C., 19, Rochester Row, London, SW 1.
† Post-war Building Studies No. 19 'Heating and Ventilation of Dwellings', H.M.S.O., 7s. 6d.

tion of the problems and requirements of domestic heating. This Report, often referred to as the *Egerton Report*, lists amongst other things the range of warmth conditions considered to be required in a house. The figures given are probably as close as one can get to 'average' conditions. They are primarily intended as a guide for heating engineers in designing heating installations. Briefly, the Report recommends that the whole house should be maintained at a temperature of at least 45° to 50° F. For living-rooms (i.e. where one is likely to be sitting down for long periods) an equivalent temperature of 62° to 66° F is recommended, for bedrooms, halls and passages 50° to 55° F and for kitchens 60° F. Conditions of comfort are not necessarily achieved merely by producing a given temperature as measured on an ordinary room thermometer. Human comfort involves other factors, such as air movement. The term *equivalent temperature* is the name given to a conception devised to provide a basis for estimating comfort conditions. It attempts to combine the effect of air temperature, radiation, and air movement (but not humidity). Methods exist for measuring the equivalent temperature.

In 1961 a sub-committee appointed by the Central Housing Advisory Committee, recommended minimum temperatures of 65° F for living areas and 55° F for circulation areas when the outside temperature is 30° F.*

It must be emphasized, however, that warmth conditions cannot be assessed in terms of temperature alone. Air temperature, air movement, humidity, and radiation from the surroundings all affect the feeling of warmth.

In any heated building the heat is eventually lost to the colder air outside by passing through the structure of the building, through cracks around windows and doors, and as the result of ventilation. To maintain the desired warmth conditions, this heat must be replaced. It stands to reason, however, that to obtain maximum economy and efficiency from any heating system the rate of heat loss should be kept to the minimum. The first step in heating a house is to ensure that there is adequate thermal insulation to prevent excessive heat loss (see chapter 10).

* 'Homes for Today and Tomorrow', H.M.S.O., 4s.

Forms of heat

Basically there are two ways in which heat is distributed: (*a*) by radiation and (*b*) by convection. Radiant heat does not warm the air. Solid objects absorb or reflect it according to their physical characteristics. It is possible to obtain comfort conditions with lower air temperatures than would be necessary when heating by convection.

Convection means that the air itself is warmed. The warmed air rises, having been displaced by the colder (i.e. denser) air and this sets up convection currents which transfer heat to the walls and ceiling of the room and to the objects within it. The air temperature is always higher than the temperature of surfaces in contact with the air, the reverse being the case with radiant heating. If the air temperature is very much higher than the mean radiant temperature of its surroundings, an atmosphere of stuffiness may result. Hence this is one more reason for adequate thermal insulation in order to ensure that walls and ceilings do not lose their heat to the outside air too quickly.

The fuel

Whatever system of heating is employed, the fuel is a basic part. The four major fuels used in this country are solid fuel (coal, coke, and specially prepared fuels such as 'Phurnacite'), gas, oil, and electricity. Wood, peat, and bottled gas are also used, but, by comparison, to a much lesser extent. In choosing a fuel most people will be vitally concerned with running costs and these are dealt with later. Apart from running costs a number of factors will influence choice, for instance availability. Each fuel has its peculiar advantages and disadvantages and the relative importance given to each depends very much on the individual. If, for example, you do not like handling fuel or ash, you would presumably not choose solid fuel. On the other hand one advantage of solid fuel is that it is suitable for a wide variety of multi-purpose appliances.

Running costs

In comparing the running costs of different fuels, it is important to use figures for the *cost per useful therm*.* This is calculated from the calorific value of the fuel, its cost, and the thermal efficiency of the appliance. An independent study of running costs was published in the Consumers' Association's journal, *Which?*, for January 1960.

Heating systems

Choice of heating system – that is, the means of providing and distributing the heat – depends on many factors: the individual requirements of the household in terms of the amount of heat and degree of control required, the cost one is prepared to pay for heating, availability of fuels, type and construction of house, whether a combined heating and hot water system is required, and so on.

In broad terms heating systems may be classified as whole house heating, partial heating, and local heating (room heaters).

Whole house heating

The term *central heating* is popularly used to describe whole house heating or partial heating. It means, literally, heating the house from a central source, i.e. the boiler. These days the term is somewhat misleading as whole house heating can be achieved by other means such as electric floor warming and electric block storage heaters.

Whole house heating systems are usually (*a*) circulated hot water; (*b*) warm air, (*c*) electric storage heaters, or (*d*) electric floor warming.

Circulated hot water heating

A boiler, either solid fuel, gas- or oil-fired, heats the water which

* A therm of heat equals 100,000 British thermal units (B.Th.U.), which is the quantity of heat required to raise the temperature of 1 lb of water through 1° F.

then circulates throughout the house by means of distributing pipework to a number of radiators or convectors. In a *gravity circulation* system, operation is based on the principle that hot water moving from the boiler in the *flow* pipes, being lighter per unit volume, will rise above the cooler water in the *return* pipes. The circulation piping must be of sufficient diameter to permit the force thus created to overcome all resistance due to friction, bends, elbows, etc. The flow pipe should rise as directly as possible from the boiler to its greatest height and then start to drop. Horizontal runs of pipe should all have a downward slope in the direction of the return to the boiler.

These days the principle of circulation by gravity has largely been superseded by what is often referred to as the *small bore* piping or *forced circulation* system in which circulation of the water is by means of an electrically operated pump (or *accelerator* as it is sometimes called). This enables much smaller bore (diameter) pipes to be used than in a gravity circulation system. Pipe diameters of $\frac{1}{2}$ in. are quite usual. The system has distinct advantages when installed in an existing house as installation is much simpler than with the larger pipes of a gravity circulation system, and making good and redecoration are reduced to a minimum. It also has the advantage of a smaller water capacity and, therefore, quicker circulation, and this leads to better response to controls and more economical working. Either system can combine hot water supply with heating (see chapter 8).

Essentially a circulated hot water small bore heating system comprises a boiler, a cylinder, a pump, the circulating pipes, and radiators or convectors.

THE BOILER

Generally speaking the heating and hot water requirements of a single family house do not require a boiler of heat rating in excess of 150,000 B.Th.U. per hour and the dividing line between the domestic and the commercial or industrial ranges of boiler is usually taken by manufacturers at about this point. Because most domestic boilers are on view in the house and are often intended to be installed in the kitchen alongside other equipment, manufacturers have in recent years made considerable efforts to produce designs which are of good appearance. Apart from the tell-tale flue, some models are difficult to distinguish from the family washing machine or refrigerator.

Solid fuel, gas- and oil-fired boilers all require flues. The manufacturer of the boiler will usually give advice about this. Generally speaking the best construction for a flue is brick. The flue should be lined internally with either salt glazed ware or asbestos cement pipes. The ideal position for it is in the centre of the house or at least on an inside wall. In this position the flue is not likely to be chilled, which could lead to condensation. Also any heat lost from it will help to warm the building. If central heating is to be installed in an old house and the existing flue has no proper lining, it is possible to insert one in the form of lead-lined flexible ducting.

There is some variation in the output efficiencies which can be expected of boilers. As a rough guide, purpose designed oil- and gas-fired boilers usually have efficiencies in the range of 75 to 80 per cent. The smaller solid fuel boilers with ratings up to 30,000 B.Th.U. per hour are around 60 per cent, the larger domestic models between 60 and 65 per cent, and the gravity-feed types up to 75 per cent. Unfortunately efficiencies as quoted by manufacturers are often *test bench* efficiencies which would not necessarily obtain in normal working conditions.

(*a*) **Solid fuel boilers.** The smallest domestic boilers (cast iron) are intended primarily for hot water supply but can usually heat a few radiators. They are within the range of 12,000 to 30,000 B.Th.U. per hour rated output. There are two main types of which in one the front may be opened to provide additional radiation to the room, while in the other the front is closed.

In post-war years a considerable improvement has taken place in the design of what are still, fundamentally, the pre-war small pot boilers. It is now usual to have controlled rates of combustion, thermostatically controlled water flow temperatures, and longer burning periods between fuelling and ashing. There are numerous makes available varying in types of grate bottom, thermostat, and air control. A few, while similar in design to the old cast iron pot boiler, are now of welded construction.

As a guide to fuel consumption, a 30,000 B.Th.U. per hour boiler of this type serving a 40-gallon water storage cylinder and

80 sq. ft of radiation surface requires $4\frac{1}{2}$ tons of coke per year for a 50-week hot water and 30-week heating season.

Sectional boilers (cast iron) were designed originally for space heating but are now often used for combined space heating and hot water supply with an indirect cylinder. They are made with casings suitable for use in the house or with plain galvanized steel insulated casings or plastic insulation intended for installing in a boiler house. Their ratings are from 30,000 B.Th.U. per hour upwards. They are fitted with thermostatic control of the primary air intake and flue damper controls are available.

As a guide for fuel consumption, a 50,000 B.Th.U. per hour boiler serving a 50-gallon hot water storage cylinder and 175 sq. ft of radiation surface will require 6 tons of coke per year for a 50-week hot water and a 30-week heating season.

Gravity feed boilers provide automatic temperature control and fuel feed to the fire. Fuel is placed in the hopper once or twice a day and flows by gravity through a constant width throat to the burning zone of the boiler.

Boilers of this type are of welded steel construction. Most types have the primary air for combustion coming in at a high velocity to the burning zone by a fan or by induced natural draught and this is controlled by an on/off thermostat. In practice the high velocity blast causes ash fusion. This type of boiler usually contains no bottom grate and the clinkers formed rest on the firebox floor from whence they are automatically ejected or easily removed by tongs. With a domestic or sectional boiler a modulating thermostat is used and maximum combustion temperature is lower and no clinker is formed; a grate is provided so that incombustibles can be removed as ash. All types will operate at the rated output for from 8 to 12 hours without attention and some for longer periods.

Controls available include thermostats for controlling water flow temperatures, room thermostats, and indoor/outdoor controllers (sometimes referred to as weatherstats).

(b) **Gas-fired boilers.** In the domestic range these are usually cast iron sectional or, more commonly, welded steel. The modern gas-fired boiler, once lit, is completely automatic, having a pilot jet which stays on when the gas is off and re-ignites the main supply when the automatic controls turn it on again. Control equipment is of three types: (i) a clock control which will turn the gas off at night and on again in the morning at pre-determined times; (ii) a thermostat controlling water flow temperatures, room thermostats, and, if required, an indoor/outdoor controller, and (iii) safety devices, such as a flame safety device to cut off the gas supply should the pilot jet be extinguished.

(c) **Oil-fired boilers.** These are of two main types, *vaporizing* and *atomizing*, according to the way in which they prepare fuel for combustion. The two types use different fuels. The first type may operate by natural draught or forced draught using a small electric fan. Some of the simpler designs are lit and adjusted by hand. Nowadays an increasing number of vaporizing burners operate with some form of electric ignitor. The atomizing type is fully automatic and relies on electrical ignition for the burners. Solid fuel boilers can be converted to oil-firing, though a boiler specially designed for oil-firing is more economical. Controls include room thermostats, water temperature control, and indoor/outdoor controller. Controls on the boiler itself differ somewhat between types, those on atomizing types (pressure jet burners) being rather more complex. The fully automatic burners, both vaporizing and atomizing can be operated in conjunction with time switches.

THE CYLINDER

There are two types of cylinder, direct and indirect (fig. 46). In the first type all the water heated by the boiler is stored in it and passes to the draw-off points as required. In the second type the water passing through and heated by the boiler does not mix with that which is drawn off at the taps. The heated water circulates continuously through either a spiral coil or a circular ring and the heat passes by conduction to the water in the rest of the cylinder.

In an area of hard water an indirect cylinder should be used. This is because deposits from the water, once it is heated, cause 'furring up' of the pipes. In a direct cylinder the water in the cylinder and in the boiler is constantly being replenished with the result that the deposits are being built up and the furring up process is consequently aggravated. In an indirect cylinder the heated water from the boiler only has to be replenished when, for example, the boiler has had to be drained down or losses due to leaks or evaporation from the feed tank have had to be made up. Deposits therefore are negligible. An indirect cylinder should also be used when the same boiler is used both for heating and hot water supply. The temperature of the heating circuit is not likely to be affected by a sudden heavy demand at the taps and

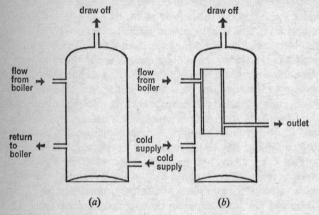

Fig. 46. Types of hot water cylinder (*a*) direct; (*b*) indirect

conversely there is not likely to be a lack of hot water for baths, etc., when a sudden outside temperature drop places a heavy load on the heating.

Cylinders are manufactured either in copper or galvanized mild steel, the manufacture of which is covered by British Standards. Choice of material for the cylinder will affect (or be affected by) choice of material for the pipes as it is inadvisable to mix materials, e.g. galvanized steel cylinder with copper pipes. The reason for this is that electrolytic action can take place when two dissimilar metals are associated with certain types of water. In the example quoted the galvanizing would deteriorate, leading ultimately to perforation of the cylinder.

THE PUMP

Most pumps used in domestic forced circulation installations are of the rotary glandless type. They can usually be supported by the pipe to which they are connected, which may be either the main flow or the main return pipe. It is advisable to have shut-off valves on both sides of the pump to facilitate servicing. The pump is operated by a small electric motor which turns a rotary impeller, which forces water through the pipes under pressure.

THE PIPES

The circulating pipes of a hot water heating system are usually either light gauge copper (to B.S.659), mild steel or wrought iron type (to B.S.1387 or B.S.788). Copper is more costly but has the advantage that it is easier to work. It is also neater in appearance and easier to paint.

The methods of jointing and supporting pipes are similar to those for the hot water and cold water plumbing.

THE RADIATORS

The *column radiator* is made of cast iron sections in a variety of heights and widths. It may be freestanding or supported on brackets built into the wall. A *panel radiator* has the waterways connected by a web of metal and is constructed either in cast iron or pressed steel. The *radiant panel heater* is a type in which hot water pipes are attached to the back of a metal panel.

THE CONVECTORS

Convectors generally work on the principle of a finned pipe set in a metal case with a damper incorporated to regulate the flow of warmed air. Air is drawn in at the bottom, passes over the finned pipe, and out through openings at the top. A further refinement is to use an electrically operated fan to force the air over the fins.

Warm air heating

The system of heating in which warmed air, not water, is circulated to provide whole house heating is less common than circulated hot water heating but is increasing in popularity. The type of system described here is the *forced* warm air type as opposed to the *gravity* type. Although common in North America, forced warm air whole house heating is still comparatively new in this country.

Basically a forced warm air system comprises a combustion unit, usually called a warm air heater, though sometimes referred to as a furnace, containing a fan which impels the heated air through ducts distributed around the house from which it is discharged through inlet grilles into the various rooms. Inlet grilles may be mounted at high or low level, but preferably at low level with return air grilles at high level. Warm air heaters may be solid fuel, gas- or oil-fired. Ducts are usually constructed of galvanized sheet steel. Concrete ducts may be used and, in fact, are necessary where they are embedded in the structure of the house (e.g. in a concrete floor), but they should be lined with a thermal insulating material. Thermostats are mounted in the rooms to control the temperature at the desired level. These are usually fixed on the wall about 5 ft above the floor and in a position not too near the source of heat or in the coldest part of the room.

Forced warm air systems may also incorporate means for providing the hot water supply, although not all warm air heaters are designed for this purpose.

Warm air heating to provide background warmth can be obtained with a type of gas convector having an electric fan which circulates warm air through ducts to other rooms.

The use of high or low level inlet grilles, provision of return air ducts, layout of ducts, choice of warm air heater, and so on are all matters on which the expert advice of an architect or heating and ventilating engineer should be obtained. Technical advice is also available from such organizations as the Gas Council, the Coal Utilization Council, and the major oil companies (see appendix 2). These bodies will also supply names and addresses of approved manufacturers and heating contractors.

Electric storage heating

Storage heaters have for some time been used in commercial and industrial premises but only recently have domestic models come on the market. A block storage heater comprises essentially a metal case containing brick or other refractory material in which is embedded the heating element. Between the brick and the metal case is a layer of insulation. Current passing through the element heats the brick. This heat is stored in the brick and gradually emitted. The principle, therefore, is one of heat storage. Heat is taken in at night during the off-peak period and emitted throughout the day.

Electricity used in ordinary convectors and radiators, whilst an efficient form of heating, is none the less expensive compared with other fuels. But used in this way, at off-peak rates, it is likely to be competitive. It is generally cheaper and easier to install than other whole house heating systems. A heater costs from about £30 and apart from this the only work is the provision of a separate electrical circuit to which all the heaters in the house must be wired. This is because the supply to the system must be separately metered as it is using electricity at the off-peak rate. Controls include a time switch, which governs the charging of the heaters and room thermostats. More refined controls which take into account the outside as well as the inside temperatures are available and are usually recommended for larger installations. Latest developments include fan assisted models in which the householder has a considerable degree of output control.

Electrical floor warming

This is also a storage system which takes advantage of the off-peak rate and has been used for some time in commercial buildings and in multi-storey blocks of flats. It consists of electric cables which are usually embedded in the concrete floor slab, so that the floor actually provides the heat storage. In some systems the cables are withdrawable, being run in conduits to which access is provided from ducts set in the floor at strategic points. This type of system can be ideal if used for background heating throughout the house with 'topping up' by individual room heaters. Its disadvantage when used on its own is that it is not a system whose output, once it is switched on, can be controlled by the householder. It is thus not able to take account of the sharp differences in temperature which so often occur in this country.

Technical advice on either system is available from the British Electrical Development Association or from the area Electricity Boards.

Partial heating

The householder who does not want whole house heating may well consider some form of partial heating. Essentially this means either background heating throughout the house (i.e. whole house heating but at a lower design temperature involving lower output ratings, hence lower installation and running costs) or the heating of some rooms or areas of the house from a central source with individual room heaters elsewhere as required. The first form, background heating throughout the house, does, of course, also require room heaters, in this case to 'top up'. Any of the systems described for whole house heating can be used for partial heating, although in some cases special versions have been designed particularly for this purpose.

Circulated hot water heating. There is a large range of solid fuel appliances on the market, in the form of open fires and openable stoves (inset or freestanding) which operate in conjunction with a *back boiler* and will heat enough water for average domestic requirements plus two or three small radiators fitted elsewhere in the house such as the hall and bedrooms. The term *back boiler* derives from the fact that these small boilers are fitted behind the appliance, actually forming the fireback in the case of open fires, and are heated by it. They are not to be confused with the larger makes of boiler known in the industry as *independent boilers* which do not operate in conjunction with a separate appliance.

Warm air heating. A form of warm air heating can be obtained with a type of gas convector having an electric fan which circulates warm air through ducts to other rooms.

Local heating

The alternative to whole house heating or partial heating is the individual room heater. There is a wide range of appliances available for all the fuels: solid fuel, gas, electricity, and paraffin. Indeed, the problem is not so much having the range from which to choose as of deciding, from a bewildering variety, the appliance which will best suit the conditions in your house, your particular requirements, and your pocket.

It goes without saying that choice of the right appliance for the room is extremely important. To most people running costs are a vital factor and these should be checked before purchasing an appliance. A number of factors influencing choice are subjective, that is they depend on the personal requirements of the householder and his family. These include convenience to the user and appearance. Probably no domestic appliance has suffered more from bad design in terms of appearance than the heating appliance, whether solid fuel, gas, electric, or paraffin. Many gas and electric appliances still attempt to imitate the traditional open fire. This is to be deplored. But there are welcome signs that visual appearance is at last beginning to catch up with the developments in functional efficiency and technical ingenuity apparent in many modern appliances. A visit to the Design Centre will bear this out.

Needless to say availability, both of appliance and fuel, must be considered and careful inquiries should be made before final choice.

Solid fuel appliances

Approved solid fuel appliances operate at efficiencies of from 35 to 70 per cent according to type of appliance and fuel. In broad terms the order of efficiency from lowest to highest is: (i) inset open fires; (ii) open fires with convection; open fires with back boilers; (iii) openable stoves; open fires with back boilers and with convection; open fires with high output back boilers; (iv) openable stoves with back boilers; (v) closed stoves. It is important, however, not to confuse efficiency with effectiveness. An appliance may be highly efficient and yet not supply enough heat for the room. This is because its rating is too low. It is far better to choose an appliance with a rating which is slightly larger than required rather than one whose rating is too low.

Inset open fire. This is the simplest type of space heating appliance and gives out heat almost entirely by radiation. The British have a traditional and understandable fondness for the open fire, though, by comparison with other forms of heating, it is not very efficient, as so much heat goes up the chimney. The modern inset open fire is a considerable improvement on its pre-war predecessor however. By providing a closely fitting ashpit cover and by sealing the joint around the firefront with asbestos string and fire cement, much greater control of combustion is possible. Efficiency may also be improved by installing a *throat restrictor* in the chimney flue. As its name implies this restricts the size of the flue opening and prevents an excessive amount of heat going up the chimney. By restricting air flow through the room and up the flue it reduces floor draughts and improves comfort conditions.

Open fire with convection. In addition to the heat given off by the fire itself in this type of appliance, air passes around behind the fireback, is thus heated, and circulates by natural convection around the room. In certain cases the warmed air can also be passed through ducts to other rooms.

Freestanding open fire with convection. It is often difficult to build in a new inset open fire into an existing fireplace opening. The tiled surround may have to be replaced and structural alterations may be necessary. To overcome these problems and hence reduce installation costs a type of open fire is available which is to all intents and purposes freestanding. There are a number of designs which differ somewhat in their method of installation relative to the existing fireplace. Some are pushed into the opening and utilize the space between the existing fireback and the back of the appliance to form a convection chamber, these are known as 'single case' convectors. Another design incorporates the convector chamber and pushes right into the existing opening, not requiring any space behind for warming convector air ('double case' convector). It is advisable to consider carefully all the available types before deciding which will best suit the fireplace conditions in your own house.

Open fire with back boiler. The practice of installing a back boiler with an inset open fire has proven very popular in local authority housing since the war. The modern inset fire used with a back boiler is generally similar to the type (see above) which does not incorporate one. Almost always, however, it has a larger firebox. The reasons for this are that (*a*) the fire may be kept alight overnight to ensure hot water in the morning, and (*b*) this type of appliance tends to burn at a higher rate. A 16-in. model should be adequate for a 30-gallon cylinder.

Since the war models have been introduced which have a large back boiler which covers the whole of the back of the fire and sometimes the sides also and often have an additional flueway through the boiler itself. This type of appliance is intended to supply from one to three radiators (depending on their size) elsewhere in the house, as well as heating the room in which it is installed and supplying a 30-gallon hot water cylinder.

Openable stove. This type of appliance is intended to satisfy the psychological need for an open fire whilst at the same time achieving a much higher efficiency. It is similar in appearance to the closed stove, and has a pair of doors which can be opened exposing the fire. This causes a slight drop in efficiency. Openable stoves are available with back boilers.

Closed stove. Of all solid fuel room heaters this is the most efficient. The fire is completely enclosed within a specially designed casing and there are no doors which can be opened to reduce the effectiveness of the 'pull' on the fire. It is essential to use smokeless fuels otherwise the flueways within the stove would be blocked with soot. Closed stoves are available in sizes suitable for heating rooms from 1,500 to 6,000 cu. ft. For a room larger than, say, 3,500 cu. ft, careful thought should be given to siting the stove in a reasonably central position, otherwise one end of the room may become overheated and the other end underheated. Closed stoves are available with back boilers. This type of stove generally incorporates a fuel hopper to give long periods of burning between refuelling.

GAS IGNITION

All inset open fires and many convector open fires are available with a gas burner to facilitate lighting the fire. This is generally a tube fixed under the grate along the front of the appliance and having jets which project a flame to the base of the fire. Gas ignition is definitely an advantage if hard coke or gas coke are used. These fuels have a high thermal efficiency but are more difficult to ignite than house coal and the reactive smokeless fuels.

Installing solid fuel appliances

For a solid fuel heating appliance to perform effectively it must be not only correctly chosen for its job but also properly installed. For example, if certain joints between an appliance and its setting are not sealed against air leaks, it may not be possible to control the fire. Leaks in joints in the flue pipe connecting a convector type of appliance with the chimney may permit warm air to be drawn into the chimney instead of flowing out into the room. The following notes are a general guide to correct fixing. They are not intended as a substitute for the manufacturer's instructions which should always be carefully followed.

GENERAL REQUIREMENTS

The fireplace opening. Take the elementary precaution, before ordering a new appliance, of ensuring that the fireplace opening is big enough or can be altered to accommodate the appliance. The manufacturer's fixing instructions should give the dimensions of opening required.

The hearth. This must be level so that the appliance, when installed, will be firm and plumb. If a new hearth is required, it should be a minimum of 6 ins. thick, should extend at least 9 ins. beyond the fireplace opening on either side, and should be not less than 16 ins. beyond the front of the appliance or the jambs of the opening, whichever projects further (fig. 47). If you have chosen a free-standing appliance to be fixed in front of the fireplace opening, the existing hearth may need to be extended.

The flue. If the chimney is sluggish, subject to down draught, or is otherwise defective, do not expect a new appliance to overcome these faults. See page 164 for the procedure for remedying chimney defects.

Hot water supply. For an appliance with a back boiler it is usually
advisable to pass pipes through sleeves when built into brickwork.
Sleeves are short sections of metal pipe of a slightly larger diameter
than the water pipes which pass through them. Never pass pipes

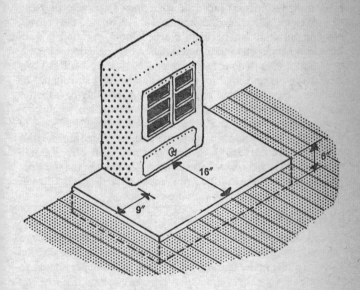

Fig. 47. Dimensions of the hearth

through a flue. Make all pipe connexions with a jointing compound
which does not set hard so that the joints can be broken easily if the
boiler has to be removed for cleaning or replacement. Fit a drain
cock with hose connexion to the lowest part of the return pipe so
the system can be emptied. The flow and return pipes should be
properly lagged.

OPEN FIRE

It is important that the existing fireback be in good condition.
Assemble the new grate and place it in position. There should be a
gap of not more than about $\frac{1}{4}$ in. between the fireback and the grate

to allow for expansion. The ends of the firebars of some appliances are notched so that they may be snapped off where necessary. This must be done very carefully to avoid snapping off too much or breaking the whole grate. If the grate is held firmly on a hard surface with the notches immediately over the edge, they can be broken off by a smart tap with a hammer. Otherwise they can be broken off with a hammer and cold chisel. Should the fireback be of an unsuitable shape, badly cracked, loose, or pitted, it is advisable to hack it out and fit a new one. A sectional fireback, of 2, 4, or 6 pieces, is preferable to a one-piece type as it is less likely to crack in use and is easier to fit into an existing surround. The sections should be jointed in fire cement or, preferably, flat asbestos tape, and the space behind the fireback filled with lightweight concrete or lime mortar during assembly. An expansion joint of strawboard or corrugated cardboard should be placed immediately behind the bottom back brick. The bottom of the fire front should be sealed at the hearth with fire cement. The sides of the fire front should be sealed against the front edges of the fireback with soft asbestos string pointed up with fire cement.

OPEN FIRE WITH BACK BOILER

The existing fireback must be hacked out as the back boiler has a fireback incorporating a specially designed boiler flue. The position and size of the boiler flue and the position of the boiler relative to the grate are very important as they have an effect on the performance of the appliance. It is desirable, therefore, to choose an appliance which is supplied as a completely assembled unit. It is not advisable to use any boiler or other component which differs from those recommended by the manufacturer. The grate must be rigidly fixed to the hearth and sealed as described for the open fire.

INSET CONVECTOR OPEN FIRE

When installing a 'single case' convector it is essential that the fireplace opening be the right size for the appliance: if it is too large the air will not be warmed enough, if too small it will not induce the necessary flow of air. The top of the convection chamber is usually formed with a special precast concrete lintel. It must be just above the warm air outlet grille when the surround is in place. A chase must be cut at the base of the brickwork at each side of the opening to take the air from the inlet grille to the convection chamber. The flue connexions must be completely sealed with soft asbestos rope and fire cement held in place by a clamping ring, otherwise the warmed air will be sucked up the chimney, or flue gases drawn into the room with the warmed air. For the same reason flow and return pipes to the boiler, if any, should be sealed at the points where they pass through the casing of the fire. The fireplace surround, fitted last, should be sealed with asbestos string along the top and the sides. It should be fixed for easy removal to allow access for inspection and maintenance of the boiler, piping, and flue connexions.

The 'double case' type of convector is somewhat easier to instal. This type is usually intended to heat a room upstairs as well and this is generally done by means of ducts, carried up from either side of the flue. The space between the outer metal casing and the brickwork should be filled with a fireproof loose-fill insulating material, such as one of the mineral wools, to reduce heat loss from the warmed air.

Another 'double case' type is one in which the warmed air is intended for return to the same room. This type not only has its own convector casing but also its own inlet and outlet grilles, making installation very much simpler. Those intended for a 16-in. or 18-in. opening are very suitable for existing fireplaces as they can often be fixed without alteration to the surround and, in some cases, without even having to remove the existing fireback.

OPENABLE STOVE

Some appliances (e.g. free-standing models) have the flue outlet at the back. If it is proposed to stand the appliance in front of an existing fireplace opening a cover plate must be fitted over the opening. This should be 20 s.w.g. sheet metal cut to shape and size and with a flue hole cut out in the required position. A short length of metal pipe must be taken from the appliance to pass through the cover plate. Having passed through, it should stop at least 4 ins. from the fireback. It is essential for the cover plate to fit tightly against the surround and for the joints to be completely sealed. There are several ways of doing this but, as it is necessary to be able to remove the cover plate from time to time in order to sweep the chimney, the following method, recommended by the Coal

Utilization Council, is probably the best, though not, of course, the cheapest. An iron frame in three parts (one for either side and one for the top), 2 ins. wide by $\frac{1}{8}$ in. thick, should be forced into the gap between the fireback and the surround and sealed in position with asbestos string and fire cement. The frame should be drilled and tapped and the cover plate screwed to it using thin asbestos string to seal the joint.

An alternative method is to brick up the opening and fit a cast iron flue box. Such a box is usually square or rectangular and has a flue socket in a plate which either hangs by lugs on the frame or is screwed directly to it. Some such frames are quite large, enabling most of the fireplace opening to be exposed when chimney sweeping. Other types are quite small and it is advisable to fill up the space behind the brickwork so that soot cannot accumulate which would be difficult to remove.

In positioning the stove there should be a minimum gap of 1 in. between the back of it and the cover plate or brickwork at the fireplace opening. If the stove is fitted hard against the cover plate, the slightest leak around the flue pipe will allow much of the warm air to be drawn into the flue, in spite of the outlet holes in the stove casing. Also heat can be lost by conduction from the stove through the metal cover plate if the two touch.

The building by-laws (Model By-laws, Series IV, Buildings, H.M.S.O., 4s.) for England and Wales specify minimum dimensions for a hearth. If the placing of a new appliance in front of an existing fireplace opening necessitates extending the hearth in order to comply with the by-laws, it may be better to fit the appliance into the fireplace opening. To do this, the best type of appliance is one with a top flue outlet. Ideally the top of the fireplace opening, where the gathering for the flue commences, should be closed off with a precast concrete unit with a hole in it to pass the flue pipe through. If this is not feasible, a stout sheet metal plate may be used, but it must be securely held in position and sealed off at the junction with the brickwork all round. The flue pipe from the stove should pass through this plate, be held in position with a clamping ring, and the joint sealed with asbestos rope.

A stove with a back flue outlet can also be fitted into a fireplace opening but it is obvious that it cannot be set as far back into the opening as a top outlet type.

INSET OPENABLE STOVE

The method of installing this type of appliance is similar to that for an inset convector open fire ('single case' type), described on page 150. It is important to seal the flue connexions properly, otherwise warmed air may be sucked into the flue or flue gases drawn into the room with the warmed air.

OTHER APPLIANCES

Independent boilers and cookers are usually quite simple to instal. A proper seal at all flue pipe connexions is essential. Soft asbestos rope, about ¾ in. diameter, wound round the pipe, tamped well into the joint, and pointed with fire cement, is the most effective way to do this. Where the pipe passes through a metal cover plate a clamping ring should be used to hold the packing in place.

When an independent boiler or other appliance with back boiler is installed in a recess, make sure that there is sufficient access for descaling the boiler.

Gas appliances

Gas room heaters fall into two categories: those with flues and those without. The following are those with flues:

Radiant fires. There are several types which give principally radiant heat. The *hearth* types have refractory elements which are heated to incandescence so that high temperature radiant heat is emitted. They are most suited to intermittent heating as their high heat output is available quite quickly after lighting and they can be adjusted to any desired temperature. Sizes available are from 16,000 to 18,000 B.Th.U. per hour input ratings. *Panel* types are similar to hearth types but are designed to be fitted into a recessed concrete block. They are more suited for building in to new houses than existing ones. *Portable hearth* fires are designed to stand freely on an existing hearth and to discharge into an existing flue. They are connected to the gas supply by means of flexible tube. Heat is mainly radiant but some convected heat is derived from the surfaces of the casing. Sizes are from 10,000 to 12,500 B.Th.U. per hour.

There is one make of combined coke and gas fire (fig. 49)

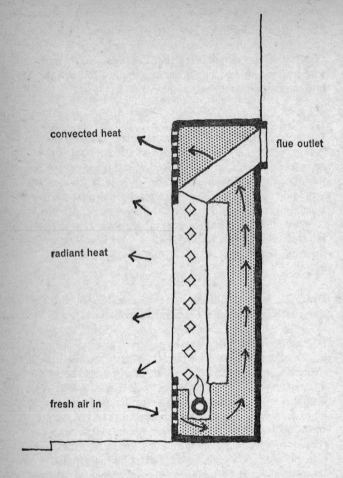

Fig. 48. Principle of operation of a gas convector heater

available in which the coke grate and gas fire use a single flue. The gas fire provides a measure of flexibility in use, such as in mild weather or late in the evening when it is not desired to refuel the coke grate.

Convector fires. These appliances actually combine radiant and convected heating. Nearly all hearth and panel heaters are of this

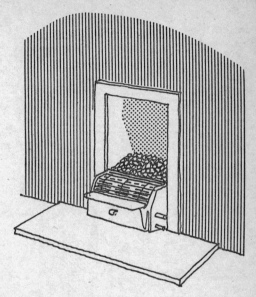

Fig. 49. Combined coke and gas fire

type. The principle of operation is similar to that illustrated in fig. 48. They operate at a slightly lower fuel consumption than radiant fires.

Balanced flue heaters. This is a type of gas appliance in which the air for combustion and the products of combustion both use the same flue, although they do not mix, of course (fig. 50). The air inlet and the flue terminal are at the same point so that any wind condition affects both equally, hence the term 'balanced flue'. All gas and solid fuel appliances require an adequate supply of air for combustion. This is usually obtained from the normal ventilation of the room. The advantage of the balanced flue heater is that it has its own air supply drawn direct from outside. Heat output is almost wholly by convection. The heaters would normally be fixed on external walls, and they are particularly suited to providing background heating. Sizes range from 10,000 to 31,500 B.Th.U. per hour.

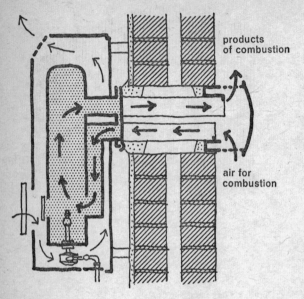

Fig. 50. Balanced flue heater: principle of operation

Convector heaters with fan-circulated warm air. These heaters, known as warm air heaters, have an electric fan which provides circulation of the warmed air. They are primarily intended for large rooms in which a single appliance is unlikely to be adequate, but they can be used with ducts to transfer heat to adjacent rooms. It is possible to have thermostatic control. Sizes range from 17,000 to 20,000 B.Th.U. per hour.

FLUELESS HEATERS

Gas heaters for use without flues are available in a number of models. Portable free-standing heaters are of the bowl reflector type. They are connected to the gas supply by means of flexible tube. Fixed flueless heaters are suitable for halls and as background heaters in large rooms.

Electric appliances

Radiant heaters. There are two forms of electric radiant heaters: the reflector type and the fire-bar type. Heat is produced by a resistance wire which glows red hot. In the reflector type this wire is wound on a rod or tube set in front of a polished metal reflector. In the fire-bar type the resistance wire is wound into a spiral and laid in grooves formed in the surface of a fireclay holder, which is heated up by the wire and emits radiant heat. The reflector type emits more radiant heat than the fire-bar type and is eminently suited to occasions when a quick response is required. It reaches its maximum heat output within two minutes of switching on. The fire-bar type takes longer but distributes its radiant heat more widely and, in addition, provides convected heat. Radiant heaters are available in a range of sizes up to 3 kW.

Radiant panel heaters. This is a type of heater suited for background heating. The surface temperature is not sufficiently high to cause discomfort if accidently touched. There are several types on the market.

Convection heaters. These consist generally of a metal or plastic case containing a heating element. Cool air is drawn in at floor level, passes over the heating element, and discharges through a grille at the top. They may be thermostatically controlled. Models are available incorporating a fan to impel the air. Both fixed and portable varieties are available in a range of sizes up to 3 kW. Convectors do not have the rapid response of radiant fires and are really intended for heating over longer periods. They would be very suitable in halls, for example, or in rooms where background heating was required.

Heaters which emit both radiant and convected heat are also available.

Tubular heaters. These consist of a steel tube, either circular or oval-shaped in cross section, at the centre of which is a heating element with a loading of 60 watts per foot run. Tubes, which may be mounted singly or in banks, are usually fixed to the wall about 4 ins. above the floor. They give off mainly convected heat and are suited, therefore, to heating for long periods. They are not particularly suitable for living-rooms, however, as a considerable length would be required to provide the necessary amount of heat. They are effective in counteracting down draughts from rooflights and clerestory windows. Lengths of from 2 ft to 17 ft in multiples of one foot are available.

Skirting heaters. These comprise a casing of sheet metal enclosing an element. Air is drawn in through inlets, passes over the element, and discharges through outlets. Loadings up to 120 watts per foot run are usual.

Infra-red heaters. These are usually designed for wall mounting although portable models are available. Unlike radiant heaters, infra-red heaters have their element wound inside a quartz tube instead of outside the tube. They are supposed to heat a greater area of a room with even heat than do radiant reflector heaters.

Liquid filled radiators. These are similar in appearance to the hot water radiator, but instead of having flow and return pipes they are merely connected to a socket outlet. The pressed steel radiator casing is hermetically sealed and contains an element immersed in liquid. The element heats the liquid which, in turn, transmits heat to the radiator. The most suitable position for such radiators is under windows. Most models have a thermostat which controls the temperature of the liquid and some models are available in which the thermostat reacts to the room air temperature.

Paraffin heaters

Portable paraffin heaters are generally of two types: the wick burner type and the concentric drum burner type. The former usually has a circular wick above which is a circular metal disc for spreading the flame. When properly adjusted it should burn with a blue flame. The wick and paraffin reservoir are housed in a sheet metal casing and the heat given off is mostly in the form of convected air from the casing.

The concentric drum burner type consists of a number of circular troughs and perforated steel drums (fig. 51). Small wicks are fitted at the base of these drums and are used for lighting the burner. The perforated drums cause a chimney effect: air is drawn through the holes and mixes with the vaporized fuel. The flame is bluish in colour and occurs mainly within and near the top of the burner. Some models have a wire mesh over the burner which becomes red

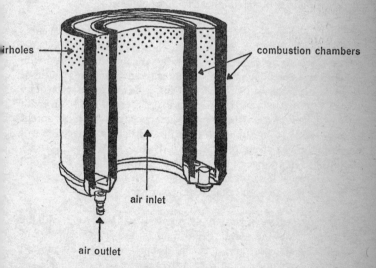

Fig. 51. Concentric drum paraffin burner

hot. Behind this is a polished metal reflector enabling a certain amount of radiant heat to be given off. Fuel consumption is around one gallon per 24 hours if properly adjusted, and heat output is nearly equivalent to a 2-kW electric heater.

Fixed heaters are also available intended for connecting to a flue. They give off convected heat. It is possible to provide a fairly extensive measure of house heating from individual flued heaters mounted in each room and all connected to and fed from an oil storage tank located outside the house. Oil is piped from the storage tank to each heater. This method of heating appears to be increasing in popularity.

Determining the size of room heater

There is no absolute method of determining the correct size (i.e. output) of heater for a room as factors such as aspect, room exposure, and construction must be taken into account and these vary considerably. The following notes may be taken as a guide. In any case the advice of the supplier should be obtained.

Solid fuel appliances. The room should be measured and its cubic content (length × width × ceiling height) obtained. Solid fuel room heating appliances are generally rated in terms of maximum room size. Inset open fires are manufactured in standard widths of 14 ins., 16 ins., and 18 ins. A fire 16 ins. wide will heat a room of up to 1,750 cu. ft, a fire 18 ins. wide up to 2,000 cu. ft. The 14 in. width is intended for use in bedrooms where most people would accept a lower level of heat output. Inset open fires with convection will warm a room of up to 2,250 cu. ft. Freestanding convectors are available in a range of sizes suitable for rooms of 1,500 to 3,000 cu. ft. Openable stoves and closed stoves are manufactured in sizes suitable for rooms of 1,500 cu. ft upwards.

Gas room heaters. If you supply your local gas showroom with the dimensions of the room, they will advise the appropriate size of appliance. If necessary, a technical representative will call and inspect the room before advice is given.

Electric fires. These are rated in kilowatts and are available in a range of sizes. The chart below (fig. 52) gives recommended ratings according to the floor area of the room.

Draw a line from the appropriate floor area on the horizontal scale to meet A-A or B-B as necessary. The required load is given on the vertical scale. Always choose the next standard size *above* the load.

A-A relates to ground-floor rooms of average pre-war construction: two external walls, area of windows not exceeding 20 per cent of floor area, ceiling height 8 ft. B-B is the same, but with one external wall only. For an average house of post-war construction the value given by A-A and B-B may be reduced by about 20 per cent.

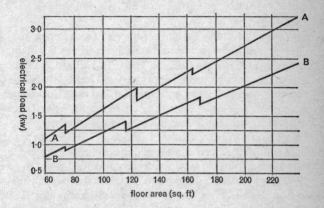

Fig. 52. Chart for determining size of electric heater for rooms of various sizes

Paraffin heaters. There does not appear to be a standard method of rating paraffin room heaters. If they are quoted by their manufacturers as being capable of heating a space of a given cubic content, they can be chosen as for solid fuel appliances described above. If quoted as equivalent to an electric fire of a given rating, the chart may be used. Some manufacturers give the fuel consumption per hour. This can be related to the electric fires chart by reckoning that $\frac{1}{8}$ of a pint of paraffin burnt every hour is equivalent to the output of a little more than that of a 1-kW. electric fire.

Fuel storage and supply

Solid fuel. The following bulk densities of various fuels may be taken as a guide in determining the amount of fuel storage required.

T – F

Coal	50 cu. ft per ton
Anthracite	50
'Phurnacite'	50
Gas coke	90*
Hard coke	90*
'Coalite'	90
'Rexco'	90

A simple fuel store may be built in the garden. It is possible to purchase prefabricated fuel stores, of which details may be obtained from the Coal Utilization Council. The Coal Utilization Council recommends a minimum storage capacity of $1\frac{1}{2}$ tons, divided into two compartments of $\frac{3}{4}$ ton each for coal and other fuel respectively (fig. 53). This is somewhat larger than those used in the construction of fuel stores in local authority houses and flats.

It must be remembered that solid fuel delivery to houses in this country is still very much of a manual operation. It is important, therefore, when considering a site for a garden fuel store, to give careful thought to the route and distance which the coalman has to come from his van. The more awkward and lengthy this is, the greater the likelihood of bumped and damaged paintwork, spilt coal, and a generally inefficient service.

Oil. Oil used for oil-fired boilers must be stored on the premises. Storage tanks are constructed of welded mild steel plates. There is a British Standard (B.S.799) which sets down standards of manufacture. Some local authorities have regulations of their own. The tank may be placed outside the house, or inside, in which case it must be in a room of its own and surrounded by a catchpit, which is a low wall of brickwork or concrete around the tank to contain the oil in case of a leak. It is generally cheaper and better to have the tank outside, where, in any case, it is likely to be more accessible to the oil supplier. A tank installed outside the house requires no protection other than painting. Some local authorities insist that it be set in a catchpit, but this is not customary in domestic installations. It should be placed preferably against a wall, not under a window if this can be avoided. Ground which falls away from the house is an ideal site as any oil spilling from the tank will

* Different cokes vary in bulk density from 75 to 112 cu. ft per ton.

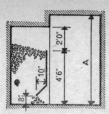

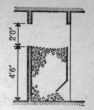

section: delivery to back of stove

section: delivery to front of stove

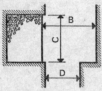

plan: delivery to front of stove

Fig. 53. Recommended dimensions for a fuel store

A Minimum head room of all passage ways, corridors and stairs used by
   the carman = 7ft 6in.
B Minimum clear width of corridor at opening to fuel store = 4ft 8in.
C Minimum clear width of delivery opening = 2ft
D Minimum clear width of all passage ways, corridors and stairs used by
   the carman = 3ft

not run back towards the house. Some tanks are supplied with
their own supports, otherwise the tank must be mounted on a
brick base.

Standard tanks are available from 50 gallons capacity upwards.
As the price of oil varies with the size of delivery the larger the tank
the cheaper the fuel. Deliveries of from 40 to 199 gallons are at one
price, those from 200 to 499 gallons at a slightly lower price, and
those from 500 gallons upwards at a lower price still. As a general
guide to the size of storage tanks the overleaf table gives tank
capacities related to boiler output rating.

The tank should be set at a slight tilt from supply pipe end to
drain valve. It should be fitted with a gauge, a drain cock, and a
boss to receive the oil supply pipe. Some tanks are also fitted with a
vent pipe.

To maintain the oil tank free from trouble ensure that:

Boiler output (B.Th.U. per hour)	Capacity (gallons)
up to 25,000*	50– 160
25,000 to 50,000	160– 275
50,000 to 100,000	275– 650
100,000 to 250,000	650–1,000

* Domestic hot water rating only. (Reproduced from the *Esso Guide to House Heating*, Section 1, Table 1·2.)

1. All caps or covers are in place and are locked or screwed home so that dirt cannot get into the oil.

2. The vent cap screen is kept clean.

3. The oil tank is filled before the house is shut up for any length of time.

4. The outside of the tank is kept painted and free from rust.

5. The drain valve is used two or three times a year to draw off any dirt or condensation which may have accumulated.

Defects and remedies

Smoky chimneys. A smoky chimney is a common complaint. The fault is seldom due to the heating appliance. Generally there are three causes which can prevent a chimney from functioning properly, apart from a build up of soot or débris. The first cause is an insufficient supply of air entering the room to replace the air going up the chimney. The second cause is poor design of the chimney and the third cause wind pressure at the top of the chimney. These causes, acting individually or together, result in smoky chimneys.

The procedure for finding and correcting the fault is one of trial and error. The first thing to be done is to have the chimney swept. If the amount of soot collected is excessive for the period since the last sweeping, the fault is probably not in the chimney but in the fuel used. For example, wood, especially when burnt green, leaves a sticky substance which is difficult to remove. Alternatively, the fault may be poor combustion in the appliance. These possibilities should be investigated before proceeding with the trials.

The flue should be carefully inspected. If the shape and position of the lintel and the size of the throat are not substantially in accordance with fig. 54, it is likely that some modifications will have to be made.

A thin sheet of metal about 6 ins. wide and slightly longer than the width of the fireplace opening is needed for carrying out the trials. If metal is not available a piece of stout cardboard will do.

When the fire is burning, open the window and door. If smoking then stops, it would appear that the fire is not getting sufficient air.

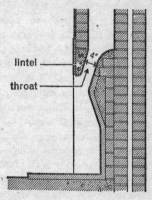

Fig 54. Section through fireplace and flue showing correct construction

As it is unlikely that you will want to leave the window or door open whilst the fire is burning, additional air must be introduced by other means. The most satisfactory way of doing this is to fit a ventilator into the external wall or into the partition wall separating the room from the hall. Alternatively, ventilators may be fitted in the floor if it is a ground floor room with a suspended timber floor. But before making permanent provision the following tests should be carried out.

1. Try the effect of reducing the height of the fireplace opening by holding or temporarily fixing a metal sheet over the top part of it. If smoking stops and the amount by which the fireplace opening is reduced is not more than 3 ins. to 4 ins. a permanent canopy should be fitted. A reduction of more than 4 ins. is likely to curtail heating of the room.

2. If, therefore, this is the case or the temporary canopy does not

stop smoking, try the effect of streamlining the entrances and reducing the throat. The opening of the throat should not exceed
40 sq. ins. in cross sectional area, except in adverse circumstances
such as top floor flats, when it may be necessary to restrict the
throat to as little as 10 to 15 sq. ins. If, by restricting the throat, an
obvious improvement is apparent, the solution will probably be to
instal a variable throat restrictor. This is an appliance, of which
there are several different types and makes on the market, which
can easily be fitted into an existing chimney.

3. Should the fire continue to smoke the cause is likely to be
difficult external conditions. Leave the throat restrictor in position
and try the effect of increasing the height of the chimney stack by
temporarily fixing a piece of sheet metal pipe on top. To make a
satisfactory test it is necessary to have two or three lengths of pipe,
starting with the shortest. When a particular length has been found
satisfactory, it will be necessary to decide whether to increase the
height of the stack or to fit a longer chimney pot.

The above assumes that the room adjoins a hall or another room
without a fireplace. If the room opens on to another room with a
fireplace and the trouble appears to be lack of air, it is more than
likely that the air for the first room is being drawn up the flue of the
second. If the two flues are in the same stack some of the smoke
issuing from the chimney of the first may be drawn down the flue
of the second room. The remedy is to leave a door or window open
in the second room or to block up the flue in this room until
required for use. The same considerations apply where the flue of
the second room comes up in the same stack as a flue from the
adjoining house.

The free-standing open fire with or without back boiler is fitted
with an adjustable throat capable of being considerably restricted.
This type of appliance, therefore, is far less likely to have smoking
troubles than are other types of open fire.

Condensation in chimneys. The following defects are frequently to
be found in or associated with chimneys:

(i) Distortion or cracking of the brickwork or masonry of the
chimney stack.

(ii) Expansion of the brickwork causing the chimney pot to sink
inside the stack.

(iii) Cracking and disintegration of render, particularly along the horizontal joints of brick chimneys.

(iv) Staining of walls and ceilings adjacent to the chimney, often accompanied by a smell.

If one or more of these defects is evident, the trouble is invariably condensation in the flue of the chimney.

The products of combustion of most fuels contain substances potentially troublesome such as sulphur compounds, ammonia, tar acids, and water vapour. These are not harmful in domestic flues as long as they remain as gases until they pass out of the flue at the top. If, however, water vapour in the gases, to take an example, condenses to liquid water before it gets out of the flue, it will be deposited on the inner surfaces of the flue, taking with it tarry substances and other matter from the flue gases. Some of the materials that thus collect on the sides of the flue are capable of absorbing moisture from the air, irrespective of whether the fire is burning or not. When condensation occurs deterioration will follow.

In the building of new houses it is possible to avoid condensation troubles by taking certain precautions:

(a) by using flue lining materials capable of resisting attack by condensate from flue gases and by providing means for collecting and removing any condensate which forms;

(b) by protecting the chimney from the entry of excessive amounts of rain;

(c) by providing adequate thermal insulation for the chimney stack.

If a chimney is so badly damaged that it requires rebuilding, then it would be sensible to ensure that the elements of good design described above are incorporated. It is not always possible or, for that matter, necessary to rebuild a damaged chimney. One method of overcoming the defect is to insert a single 6 ft length of asbestos cement pipe in the exposed part of the stack so that it reaches just below the junction of the chimney with the roof. The bottom of the pipe must be securely fixed in such a way that it will not interfere with sweeping. A method of doing this is illustrated in fig. 55. The top of the pipe should be finished off with a chimney pot in the normal way.

Where deposits from condensation have penetrated through the brickwork and stained the plaster, the first step is to prevent condensation soaking into the brickwork. This can be done by one of the methods described above. The most effective remedy is then to remove all the contaminated brickwork and plaster and replace it with new materials. If this cannot be seriously considered, the alternative is to wait for the brickwork to dry out, then treat the stained plaster by an application of two coats of a sealer such as shellac or knotting or aluminium paint. The wall should then be lined with a heavy lining paper followed by a coat of glue size. Should you not want to wait until the brickwork has thoroughly dried out before re-decoration, an alternative treatment, rather more expensive, is to fix plasterboard with an aluminium foil backing to the wall. The foil should be given a good coat of bitumen

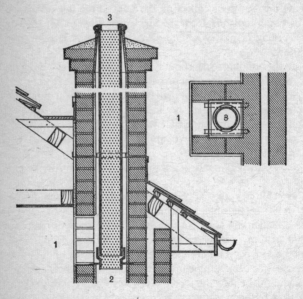

Fig. 55. Inserting a flue lining into an existing chimney

1 Remove three or four courses of bricks for access
2 Insert mild steel bars into brickwork to support asbestos cement plate
3 Insert asbestos cement lining pipe from top of chimney

paint and then fixed in contact with the wall. The exposed face of
the plasterboard is then ready for decoration.

Fuel should be stored in a dry place because if it gets wet the amount
of water vapour in it increases and can aggravate condensation
troubles in the fuel. Also, it is unwise to burn wet or damp substances such as tea leaves, potato peelings, hedge clippings, or
green wood in a boiler or other slow burning appliance.

CHAPTER 12

Electrical installation

Great Britain is served by a national electricity grid under the control of the Central Electricity Authority. Current is supplied to the Electricity Boards, of which there are fourteen throughout England, Scotland, and Wales. These area boards are the supply authorities providing the householder with his electricity. Almost all electricity is supplied at a standard 240-volt alternating current (AC), but there are still a few districts with non-standard supplies.

The following electrical terms are in common use, though frequently misunderstood.

Ampere (*amp*): the rate of flow of the current.
Volt: the unit of pressure.
Watt: the unit of power.
Unit: 1,000 Watt-hours, the rate at which electricity is consumed. A 100-watt lamp uses 1 unit in 10 hours, a 1,000-watt (1-kW) electric fire uses 1 unit in 1 hour.
Socket outlet: sometimes called a power point, is fixed to the wall and a socket plug, attached to an appliance, plugged into it.

Tariffs

Electricity used to be charged separately for lighting (at a fairly high rate) and power (at a lower rate). This meant that the lighting and power circuits had to be metered separately. Today the general method of charging is the 'two-part-tariff'. This consists of a fixed charge, based on the floor area or electricity load of the house, and a rate per unit consumed.

The installation

The electricity supply to a house is brought in either underground or overhead and there is a main fuse to which it is connected as near as possible to the point of entry into the house.

Adjacent to this is the meter and the consumer's (i.e. householder's) main switch. Everything up to and including the main fuse and meter is the property and responsibility of the supply authority; everything from this point onwards is the property and responsibility of the consumer. The main fuse is housed in a sealed box and should it 'blow', which is unlikely, the supply authority must be summoned to repair it. The consumer's main switch cuts off the supply throughout the house and should be turned off when a fuse is to be mended.

From the main switch a cable passes to a distribution board which is usually mounted on the wall nearby, although it is not essential for it to be adjacent to the main switch. The distribution board is the point from which circuits serving light and socket outlets throughout the house branch off. Fuses, one to each circuit, are mounted on the board.

It is usual to connect up to 10 light points to one circuit. The average two-storey house, therefore, would have 2 or 3 circuits for the lights. The fuses for this are 2 amp. Until the introduction of the ring circuit system described below, socket outlets were either of the 2, 5, 10, or 15 amp. 2- or 3-pin type, and in many installations each socket outlet was wired to a separate circuit. This made the provision of socket outlets relatively expensive and is the reason that most pre-war houses are provided with very few.

It is important not to overload a circuit by plugging in an appliance which exceeds the loading for a particular socket outlet. As a general guide, if you have the older type of socket outlet, connect only lamps, clocks, the radio or television set to a 2-amp. socket outlet, connect the vacuum cleaner to a 5-amp. socket outlet, and heaters to a 15-amp. socket outlet.

A fuse consists, essentially, of a wire housed in an insulated holder. When a fuse 'blows' it means that the wire has melted due to overloading. The fuse is thus a deliberate form of safety device.

These days circuit breakers are sometimes used instead of fuses. A circuit breaker is a form of switch which shuts itself off when a circuit is overloaded. If the appliance responsible for the overloading is disconnected the switch can be turned on again and will stay on, but if it shuts itself off this means that there is a defect in the circuit and an electrician should be called to examine it.

It is always advisable to keep a spare card of fuse wires, or, better still, a spare set of wired fuseways* and a torch near the fuses. Always use the correct size of fuse wire. If too small a wire is used the fuse will blow again, if too large a wire is used the circuit may become overheated and blow the supply authority's fuse or even cause a fire. Fuse wire is sold on cards marked with its amperage: the higher the amperage the thicker the wire. It is obtainable from builders' merchants, hardware shops, and chain stores such as Woolworth's.

Repairing a fuse

To repair a fuse which has blown, switch the current off at the main switch, pull out each fuse in turn and examine it for a melted wire. When the faulty one has been located, loosen the screws at both ends, extract the damaged fuse wire and insert a new wire, twining it round the screws. Tighten the screws at both ends, replace the fuse, and switch on the main switch.

To avoid having to search for the fuse it is a good idea when moving into a house to locate the fuses belonging to each circuit and to mark them on a diagram fixed near the fuseboard. To do this, switch off the current at the main switch, pull out the individual circuit fuses, switch on again, and turn on all the lights and appliances. Those that do not come on are on the disconnected circuit. Note these on the diagram and repeat the process for each circuit in turn until all have been recorded.

Ring circuit

Post-war houses and older houses which have been rewired in recent years will generally have all their socket outlets connected to a *ring circuit*. The ring circuit consists of a two-wire cable plus an earth wire and is connected to a 30-amp. switch fuse. From this it runs to *all* the socket outlets and then back to the switch fuse, thus forming a ring. Houses of a maximum floor area of 1,000 sq. ft or less are not limited in the number of socket outlets which may be connected to a ring circuit. Those exceeding 1,000 sq. ft require a further ring circuit for each successive 1,000 sq. ft. There is thus no reason why two or more ring circuits should not be provided in a

* A fuseway is the whole unit containing the fuse wire.

house, particularly when a lot of appliances are likely to be used. Additional socket outlets may be added, in which case they are connected to a *spur* from the ring circuit. Each spur may serve two 13-amp. sockets or one fixed appliance on the same size cable as that on the ring circuit. The total of all the sockets on all spurs, however, must not exceed the number of those on the ring circuit itself.

The socket outlets are rated at 3 kW (13 amp. at 230 volt) and are suitable for alternating current only. Plugs for these sockets are fitted with cartridge fuses of either 2 amp. (coloured blue), 5 amp. (grey), or 13 amp. (brown). The replacing of a fuse is a simple matter. Pull out the plug, unscrew the casing, prise out the fuse, being careful not to damage the clips, replace, and reassemble. Plugs are available with switches and these provide a cheaper alternative than the switch socket and can be fitted by the householder.

Switches

At one time the type of switch known as 'quick make and break' (Q.M.Q.B.) was in general use. This was at a time when the electricity supply in this country was on direct current (D.C.) and the Q.M.Q.B. switch was desirable in order to prevent arcing and burning of the switch contacts. The Q.M.Q.B. switch clicks distinctly when operated. If it does not do so and if the dolly* is loose the spring is broken and the switch should be replaced. Now that alternating current (A.C.) has almost completely replaced D.C. supply, slow break switches which are virtually noiseless are normally installed. In bathrooms and kitchens it is desirable to have ceiling mounted cord switches as they are safe when operated by wet hands.

Circuit wiring

Circuit wiring was at one time almost always housed in metal conduit: the wires being pulled through the conduit after it was fixed in position. One advantage of this system was that rewiring

* The dolly is the actual switch itself which you handle to turn on or off.

could be carried out merely by pulling the new wiring through the existing conduit after the old wiring had been removed. In recent years other materials have been developed such as polyvinyl chloride (P.V.C.) sheathed wiring and tough rubber sheathed (T.R.S.). Other forms of wiring include lead-covered (often found in old houses) and copper sheathed (M.I.C.C.) which is not normally used in domestic installations.

Rewiring

Electrical wiring does not last forever and sooner or later needs replacement. In the interests of safety it is wise to renew the wiring in a house once its condition starts to deteriorate. One rule when buying an old house is to have the wiring examined and tested by the supply authority.

Deterioration is likely to become evident after about 30 years, and for this reason, if you know that the wiring is of this age it is advisable to call in a reliable electrician or the supply authority to examine it.

Rewiring generally involves a certain amount of redecoration, particularly if you want it to be concealed. Most people, when about to have their houses re-wired, like to take the opportunity of having extra socket outlets or light points put in and occasionally moving the positions of existing switches and outlets. This will mean cutting new chases in the walls and then replastering and redecorating. Floorboards will have to be taken up so that wiring can be run between the floor joists to light points in the ceiling of the rooms below. Some houses have internal walls constructed of hollow blocks or timber framing, enabling wiring to be dropped down within the thickness of the wall and obviating the need for wall chases.

CHAPTER 13

Gas installation

Since 1948, the gas supply in Great Britain has been a nationalized industry and is controlled by twelve Area Gas Boards under the guidance of the Gas Council.

The great majority of gas produced in this country derives from coal, although an increasing proportion is likely in future to be obtained from oil and oil derivatives. There is not yet a national gas grid, although most boards have local grids over all or part of their areas. Gas is a highly efficient fuel both for cooking and for heating, it is clean and does not require fuel storage. Also it is backed up by a high standard of service. Advice is readily available from the Area Gas Boards.

Tariffs

The method of charging for domestic installations is known as the 'two-part' tariff. A standing charge is made, including meter rent, which is not related to gas consumed and gas is charged at a flat rate per therm, which is 100,000 B.Th.U.

The installation

The gas supply to a house comes from an underground main in the street. A service pipe, usually 1¼-in. wrought iron,

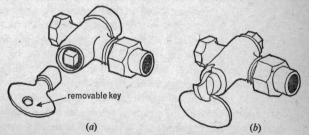

Fig. 56. Types of gas tap (*a*) nursery or lockshield; (*b*) drop fan

comes from the main, also underground, and terminates at a meter in the house. A tap is fitted to the pipe so that, in the event of a leak, this can be turned off by the householder until the gas board service department repairs the leak. This tap, called the meter control cock, also enables the gas supply to be turned off if the meter is to be exchanged or any repair or extension carried out on the house supply. From the meter, installation pipes are extended to all the points and appliances in the house. Taps on gas pipes should be of the 'drop fan' type (fig. 56). These cannot be turned on accidentally. If there is a risk of small children turning taps on, a tap of the 'nursery' or 'lockshield' type should be used.

Bottled gas

In districts where a mains supply is not available bottled gas may be used. This is either butane or propane, both by-products of oil. It can be stored safely as a liquid at room temperature and released as a gas. It is stored in steel containers under a pressure of approximately 25 lb per sq. in. Sizes of container vary but a capacity corresponding to 200 cu. ft. of gas is usual. Two containers are normally used at the same time and automatic change-over switches can be fitted. Installation pipes can be smaller because of the higher calorific value of bottled gas. However, if there is the likelihood of connexion to town gas in the near future it is advisable to instal pipes which will be large enough for this purpose.

Defects and remedies

If you suspect that gas is leaking, turn off all appliances and turn off the main tap at the meter. Open all the windows. Telephone the gas board immediately and they will send someone to locate and repair the fault. Area Gas Boards treat gas escapes as requiring immediate attention and give them priority over other work.

Apart from leaks the most common defect in a gas installation is loss of pressure. This may, of course, be the result of reduced pressure in the gas mains, in which case there is not much that can be done about it. Such cases, however, are exceptional nowadays. The pipes, however, may have become coated with deposits and require cleaning out. This is done by forcing air through them, a task which the service department of the Gas Board is equipped to carry out.

Low pressure may be the result of a badly designed installation, although this is not very likely. If at some time the supply in the house has been extended without increasing the capacity of the service pipe, low pressures may result. The remedy is to replace the service pipe between main and meter with a larger diameter pipe. The piping in the house will probably also need enlarging. The replacement of the service pipe between main and meter is carried out by the gas board who make a charge for this work. For replacing gas pipes in the house a plumber and gas fitter should be employed.

The gas installation in a house cannot be expected to function forever without attention. In fact regular inspection and maintenance should be carried out at least once a year, a service which the gas board will undertake. Maintenance includes examination of taps to ensure they work easily, and of flexible tubing to ensure it is in good condition, cleaning of burners and flueways and checking of all controls of appliances and, in the case of hard water areas, the descaling of waterways in water heaters.

If you wish to alter or extend the supply in your house it is important to decide exactly what you want. Get in touch with the local area board who will send a technical representative to discuss your requirements. He will advise on all matters concerning the gas service.

CHAPTER 14

Painting and decorating

Painting and decorating have always been jobs which the amateur is prepared to tackle. High costs of labour and material since the war have encouraged even the laziest and least practical amongst us to try their hand at it. But it is wrong to assume that it is work that does not require skill and patience to produce a really good job. Skill comes only with practice but even without it a job will be improved if the following rules are conscientiously observed.

1. If possible use one manufacturer's materials only on any one surface (i.e. priming, undercoating, final coating) and follow his instructions carefully.

2. Use the type of paint and number of coats recommended by the manufacturer for the purpose you intend to use it.

3. Store paint in a dry place where frost cannot affect it.

4. Thoroughly clean down and prepare the surface to be painted.

5. Make sure that the surface is quite dry and free of dust before painting.

6. Use only good quality brushes or rollers and carefully clean them after use.

7. Stir the paint thoroughly before application (except in the case of thixotropic or jelly paints).

8. Avoid painting external surfaces during wet or damp weather.

9. Do not flood the brush with paint. In most cases $\frac{1}{2}$ in. to 1 in. of paint on the end of a brush is sufficient.

Types of paint

There has been marked progress in the development of new types of paint and in the improvement of some of the older types over the past 10 or 15 years, stimulated no doubt by the enormous increase in do-it-yourself painting and decorating. The success of a scheme of redecoration depends as much on the types of paint used as on the workmanship and care in the preparation of surfaces. Some say the type of paint is the most important element.

The formulation and manufacture of paint is a highly technical and commercially competitive field in which even experts find it difficult to keep pace with new developments. Nevertheless it is desirable for the amateur to have a general understanding of the main types or groups to which most paints belong. Later in the chapter factors to be taken into account in choosing types of paint are discussed. No attempt is made here to assess the merits of proprietary brands. A reputable manufacturer will always advise on what his paints are capable of doing and what they will not do and his advice should be followed. The Building Research Station has produced a number of digests on the subject, available generally at 4d. a copy from H.M.S.O.

Essentially paint can be said to comprise a pigment, a binding medium, and a thinner. The latter is there to make the mixture suitable for application by brush, roller, or paint spray. Once applied, paint changes from a fluid to a film which binds the pigment. The nature of the change depends on the type of paint. There are four main types or groups.

The first group comprises those paints which lose their thinner by evaporation. The resulting film, however, remains soluble in this thinner so that when further coats of the same paint are applied care must be taken not to pull up the previous coat. To this group belong bitumen, chlorinated rubber, and cellulose paints.

The second group is the oil paint group in which the binding medium is a drying oil. The change from fluid to film comes about in part by a chemical reaction with oxygen absorbed from the atmosphere. This group includes full gloss, oil gloss, and flat oil paints. Some bituminous and imitation stone paints incorporate a drying oil medium.

Thirdly there is the water paint group. The binder is emulsified, that is it is dispersed as globules in an aqueous liquid. Once the paint has been applied its water content evaporates causing the globules to coalesce and form a tough water-resistant film. Paints in this group include the various emulsion paints, oil-bound water paint, cement paint, and non-washable distemper. Some bituminous and imitation stone paints have an emulsion medium.

One of the greatest boosts to do-it-yourself painting and decorating in recent years has undoubtedly been the advent of emulsion paint. It provides a finish which is quick-drying, fairly free from smell, and easily applied. Certain types are suitable for kitchens and bathrooms and even for external walls.

Finally there is the group comprising the two-part paints. The two parts are mixed just before application and combine chemically to form a tough resinous material. This group includes the epoxy resin, polyurethane resin, and polyester resin paints.

There are special types of paint which do not necessarily conform exactly with the above categories. These include tar paints, anti-condensation paints, heat-resisting paints, and so on. The paints described above are finished coatings.

On new, previously unpainted surfaces the first coat of paint is the *primer*. Its function is to adhere firmly to the surface and provide a suitable base for the remaining coats of paint. One coat of primer is normally sufficient although in certain circumstances such as the end grain of timber it is advisable to apply two coats. After the primer comes the *undercoat*. Its chief functions are to obscure the primed surface, to provide a fresh surface of uniform texture and of a colour approaching that of the finishing coat, and to build up a layer of paint sufficient in type and thickness to protect the painted surface. At least two coats should be applied. Finally comes the *finishing* coat, which is there to provide the particular colour and texture required.

PRIMERS

As mentioned above, these have a vital part in forming a suitable base for subsequent coats of paint. There are many types of primer, each designed for a specific use: wood primers, primers for ferrous metals, primers for non-ferrous metals (e.g. aluminium), and primers for plaster surfaces. See *Preparation of surfaces*, page 188, for guidance on what type of primer to use and when.

SEALERS

A clear or pigmented liquid preparation used on absorbent surfaces to reduce porosity prior to painting; also used when necessary to prevent any soluble or diffusible matter in the surface from 'bleeding' into and disfiguring the new paint.

KNOTTING

A substance made by dissolving shellac or other resin and applied to knots in timber before painting to prevent resinous materials in the timber from passing into the paint film and causing discoloration and/or defective drying.

STOPPING

The term applied to manufactured materials containing hard-setting ingredients and used for filling holes and cracks in timber after priming.

FILLERS

The term applied to manufactured materials containing a water-soluble binder mixed with various mineral powders to which water is added to produce a workable consistency; used to fill cracks and holes in plaster surfaces. Another type of filler is used for levelling up undulations in sheet metal.

Brushes

The most important part of a brush is the hair or bristle. The best quality brushes are usually made with hog hair. For cheaper brushes horse hair is normally used, sometimes mixed with hog hair. Fibre is used in lime brushes (see below) because it is resistant to the action of alkalis. It is sometimes mixed with other hair in brushes of cheap quality. Sable, badger, ox, and camel hair are also used in brushes of various qualities but generally for special purposes such as signwriters' brushes.

There are a number of types of brush (fig. 57) used by the craftsman painter, but the amateur will generally be concerned with the following:

FLAT WALL BRUSH

As its name implies, it is used for painting large areas and is made in widths ranging from 3 ins. to 5 ins. It is generally of hog hair (best quality), horse hair, a mixture of hog and horse hair or, in the cheaper varieties, a mixture of horse hair and fibre.

PAINT OR VARNISH BRUSH

This is really a small version of the flat wall brush, being made in widths ranging from 1 in. to 3 ins.

SASH TOOL

This is a small paint brush, usually $\frac{3}{4}$ in. wide, used for window sashes, cutting in, etc.

DISTEMPER BRUSH

This is used for distempering wall and ceiling surfaces. It can also be used for applying the paste to wallpaper. An old distemper brush is very useful for washing down surfaces and for other preparation work. Distemper brushes are large: they come in widths ranging from 5 ins. to 7 ins., and the best quality are made of hog hair. They are constructed in one of two ways: either the hair is set evenly along each side of a wooden wedge for the full width and bound with leather or metal, or it is grouped into 2, 3, or 4 knots, each bound with metal or wire secured to the stock.

LIME BRUSH

This is similar in construction to a distemper brush but is generally made of fibre or coarse hair. It is used for applying lime washes, but is also a suitable tool for washing down and general preparation work.

The hair in a good quality brush will be 'springy'. It should keep its shape during use, not splay outwards for example. If the brush is well made, loose hairs will not come away during use.

Never neglect to clean a brush thoroughly after use. Brushes used in emulsion paint or distemper should be rinsed under a running cold tap and shaken dry immediately after use. Brushes used in oil paints should be cleaned with white spirit. After this first cleaning, brushes should then be washed in soap and water. If the brush is to be used again quite soon, it may be suspended in a can or jar with the bottom $\frac{1}{2}$ in. or so immersed in water.

Rollers

These are very popular with the amateur. There are several makes on the market, the roller itself being a layer of lambswool, mohair, or foam polystyrene. Basically there are two types, that in which the paint is contained within a perforated drum and soaks through into the roller material during application and that in which the paint is placed in a shallow dish and the roller worked up and down in it until it is saturated with paint. Both types function well only if properly cleaned after each use.

When applying a priming coat on a bare surface or any coat on a surface suspected of being not entirely free from dust or grease or moisture, it is preferable to use a brush rather than a roller so that the paint can be worked well into the surface.

Rollers are particularly suitable for doing large flat areas such as ceilings, and rough surfaces. Some people find them very satisfactory for painting wire fencing.

Some enthusiasts find the use of paint sprays highly satisfactory. These may be purchased at builders' merchants or even improvised from certain types of vacuum cleaner.

Other tools

Apart from brushes, painting and decorating involve the use of other tools which, if of good quality and condition and of the right type, contribute to a satisfactory job (see fig. 57).

STRIPPING KNIFE
This is used for removing wallpaper or paint. It has a stiff steel blade usually from 1 in. to 4 ins. wide.

FILLING KNIFE
This is used for applying filling to surfaces. It is similar to a stripping knife but has a more flexible blade.

STOPPING KNIFE
This is used for filling nail holes, cracks, and small apertures. It is also used for smoothing new putty in glazing. It has a fairly stiff steel blade.

SHAVE HOOK
This is used for removing paint from architraves, skirtings, and other moulded surfaces.

Choice of paint

When choosing a type of paint, it is important to consider its

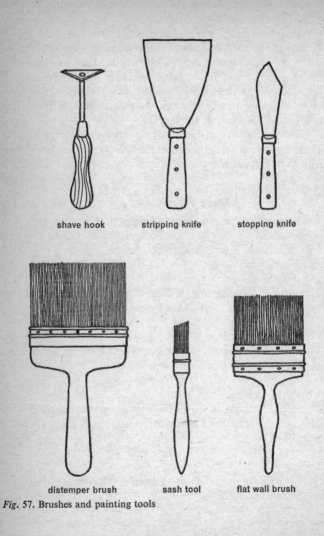

shave hook   stripping knife   stopping knife

distemper brush   sash tool   flat wall brush

Fig. 57. Brushes and painting tools

suitability for the surface. The following points should be considered.

Nature and condition of surface. These are the most important factors influencing the choice of paint. The Tables on pages 186 and 187 list types of surface (external and internal) and paints suitable for use on each surface. These tables, based on British Standard Code of Practice C.P.231 (1952), will enable you to narrow your choice. Final selection will depend upon one or more of the following.

Exposure conditions. Paints used on external surfaces generally have to contend with more severe conditions of exposure than those used inside the house. You may have internal conditions, however, which are almost as difficult. A kitchen or bathroom, for example, where there is likely to be steam and possibly some condensation, requires special consideration. A basement which is damp is another instance.

Damp and condensation are dealt with elsewhere in this book. In both cases it is obviously desirable to eliminate the problem at source, but this may often be a counsel of perfection.

Where the surface has been painted previously. Unless a previously painted surface has the old paint film (including undercoats) completely removed, it is wise to redecorate with the same type of paint. For this reason it is advisable always to keep a record of the types of paint used each time you redecorate.

Ease of re-painting. If, when next you re-paint, you want to be able to do so without stripping off the old paint film, it is advisable to avoid using distempers. An old distemper surface will not provide an adequate backing for new paint applied over it.

Ease of cleaning. This is a practical necessity if there are children in the house. Most manufacturers market a paint which is washable. Remember, however, that frequent vigorous washing down will eventually wear even some of the so-called washable paints. On woodwork, such as doors and architraves which are likely to get finger-marked, it is advisable to use a gloss or semi-gloss finish.

INTERNAL PAINTED SURFACES: SUITABLE TREATMENTS

Item	Woodwork	Fibre building board	Ironwork	Plaster walls	Plaster ceilings	Brickwork	Concrete and renderings
Living-rooms, halls, and staircases, bedrooms	Full gloss paint, oil gloss paint, stain, varnish	Flat oil paint, oil-bound water paint	Full gloss paint, oil gloss paint	Full gloss paint, varnish, flat oil paint, oil-bound water paint, emulsion paint	Flat oil paint, oil-bound water paint, non-washable distemper, emulsion paint	Oil gloss paint, flat oil paint, oil-bound water paint, emulsion paint	As for brickwork
Kitchens, sculleries, bathrooms, lavatories	Full gloss paint, stain, varnish	Full gloss paint, flat oil paint, oil-bound water paint	Full gloss paint	Full gloss paint, flat oil paint, some emulsion paints	As above	Oil gloss paint, flat oil paint, oil-bound water paint, cement paint, some emulsion paints	As for brickwork
Hot water pipes, radiators	—	—	Heat resisting paint	—	—	—	—
Floors	Stain, varnish, special floor paints, floor seals	—	—	—	—	—	—

EXTERNAL PAINTED SURFACES: SUITABLE TREATMENTS

Item	Woodwork	Ironwork	Brickwork	Stucco	Concrete Renderings
Walls and soffits	Full gloss paint, oil gloss paint, varnish	Full gloss paint, oil gloss paint	Full gloss paint, oil gloss paint, oil-bound water paint, cement paint, imitation stone paint	As for brickwork	Oil gloss paint, oil-bound water paint, cement paint, imitation stone paint
Sashes and frames	As above	As above	—	—	—
Bargeboards and similar joinery	As above	—	—	—	—
Front doors	Full gloss paint, flat oil paint	—	—	—	—
Gutters and pipes	—	Full gloss paint, oil gloss paint, bituminous paint	—	—	—
Buried ironwork	—	Bituminous paint, tar paint	—	—	—

Colours. Much can be said about the functional use of colour in the house, but it is beyond the scope of this book. For choice of colour there is a British Standard range (B.S.2660). Paints can be made up in any colour you wish or you can mix a colour yourself using stainers. Most of the larger paint manufacturers produce most, if not all, of the colours from this range.

Ease of application. With a few exceptions most paints these days are not difficult to apply. For those which are, there is usually a good reason, such as the inclusion of a constituent to provide high resistance to chemical attack. At the other extreme are the 'nondrip' paints in which the pigment or medium has been modified to make them thixotropic. These paints can be applied in heavy coats without *sagging** resulting. Emulsion paints have the attraction that brushes can be washed out in water after use. But this should never be the sole criterion for choosing such paints.

Quick drying. To minimize the period of inconvenience during redecoration, it is often desirable to use quick-drying paints. Emulsion paints require only short periods for drying out between coats and are therefore very suitable when time is a factor. There are quick-drying high gloss paints available based on specially selected thinners and media, usually modified alkyds, that is, a synthetic resin. Cellulose and similar paints are also quick drying.

Preparation of surfaces

Because it is usually hard work with little or nothing to show for it, surface preparation is often skimped. Whether or not a surface has been previously painted, it should be clean and free from grease or moisture. Failure to prepare properly before painting will generally lessen the life of the paint film.

It is important to understand the distinction between stripping and rubbing down. To strip a previously painted surface means to remove the old paint film, whether by stripping knife, chemical paint remover, or blowlamp. To rub it down means to remove loose particles of paint and to smooth the surface of paint film

---

* See list of defects, page 193.

which is adhering satisfactorily by rubbing it with sandpaper. As a general rule it is not necessary to strip off old paintwork, provided it is in reasonably sound condition and adhering to the surface. At the most it should be washed down well, using hot water and a mild detergent to remove dirt or loose substances likely to affect the adhesion of the new paint film. Soda, soft soap, and other highly alkaline soaps destroy most paints and, if used for washing down, should be well diluted. Once the dirt is loosened, wash down with plenty of clean water and allow to dry.

An exception to the rule is a surface previously painted with non-washable distemper (sometimes referred to as ceiling distemper). This should be completely removed by thorough washing down (usually requiring considerable effort) as it is not a suitable base for new paint, which will eventually tend to lift.

Never paint directly over creosote, bitumen, or tarry materials; they will 'bleed' through the new paint and discolour it. Remove as much of the creosote, etc., as possible by scraping, then re-seal with one or two coats of shellac knotting or with two coats of aluminium wood primer before repainting.

Remember, it is always better to repaint using the same type of paint as before. Any risk of incompatibility between old and new paint films is thus eliminated.

New woodwork. Punch all nail heads below the surface and apply stopping after priming; rub the surface down with sandpaper; apply a priming coat of white lead linseed oil primer or an aluminium wood primer. A leadless primer is suitable for internal woodwork but should not be used on external woodwork. If the woodwork is oily, scrub the surface with acetone, allow it to evaporate, and then treat as above. If it is resin stained, apply aluminium wood primer. Large knots should be cut out with a chisel. Otherwise treat knots with a proprietary knotting and then apply one coat of well-thinned red lead before priming.

Previously painted woodwork. If the previous paint film is in reasonably sound condition, it is not necessary to remove it. Simply rub down with an abrasive paper, clean off, and apply the paint coats. Priming is not necessary. A previously polished surface should be wiped down with a clean rag and white spirit to remove grease. If the old paint is in poor condition, it must be removed. Burning off should only be done if you are experienced at it. Inside the house it is preferable to remove paint with a proprietary paint stripper. This is simply an organic solvent (containing also waxes or thickeners to hold the solvent in contact with the surface) which swells and softens the paint, making it fairly easy to remove with a stripping knife or shave hook. If you strip back to bare woodwork, it is then necessary to prepare the surface as for new woodwork. When using a paint stripper always make sure that the room you are working in is well ventilated.

New plaster. Thoroughly brush down to remove all dirt and loose or powdery material.

Certain plasters are liable to attack paint chemically. These include lime and lime-gauged plasters and those containing portland cement products. In such cases the surface should be primed with an alkali-resistant primer if the paint to be used is an oil paint.

New plaster takes some time to dry out. Obviously the longer it is left before painting the better. If you cannot leave it until you are sure it has dried out, use a porous finish, such as emulsion paint or distemper. It is not possible to stipulate a minimum period for drying out; it depends so much on particular conditions. It is not unusual to have to allow several months.

Previously painted plaster. If the old paint film is firm, treat as for new plaster above. Otherwise wash down the surface with hot water and a mild detergent; allow to dry before painting.

New cement render or bare concrete. As for new plaster.

Previously painted cement render or bare concrete. As for previously painted plaster.

Bare brickwork. Wash down the surface or wire-brush it to remove all dirt and loose material.

Previously painted brickwork. If the old paint film is firm, treat as for bare brickwork. Otherwise wash down the surface with hot water and a mild detergent; allow to dry before painting.

New asbestos cement. Thoroughly brush down to remove all dirt and loose or powdery material. Prime with two coats of an alkali-resistant primer.

Previously painted asbestos cement. If the old paint film is firm, treat as for new asbestos cement. Otherwise use a wire brush or paint remover to remove the old paint film. If using paint remover wash it off thoroughly afterwards, otherwise it will sink into the asbestos cement. *Never* use a blow lamp as asbestos cement may crack or break up with explosive violence if overheated.

New metalwork. Galvanized iron or steel, which has not previously been painted, can be treated with one of the proprietary solutions containing phosphoric acid which are available for the purpose. Thoroughly rinse the surface after use, however. Prime with red lead, metallic lead paint, zinc chromate primer, or calcium plumbate. New zinc should be allowed to weather for some months before painting. Bright zinc must be roughened, one method being to use a proprietary solution containing phosphoric acid as above. Prime with calcium plumbate primer. New aluminium should have all oil or grease removed. This can be done by swabbing it with a solvent comprising a mixture of equal parts of white spirit and solvent naptha. If the surface is highly polished, apply a proprietary etching liquid after degreasing to provide a key for paint. Rinse the metal thoroughly and allow to dry before painting. Prime with zinc chromate primer.

The inside of galvanized steel cisterns can be protected against corrosion by painting with bituminous paint. Several makes are available which do not taint water.

Previously painted metalwork. If rust is present, which is very likely, it must be completely removed by scraping or with a blow lamp. It should then be primed as above.

Wallpaper. There is no reason why old wallpaper should not provide a perfectly sound base on which to paint. Indeed, in many very old houses, it may be advisable not to attempt to remove the wallpaper because of the possibly poor condition of the plaster underneath. If the wallpaper is adhering well, wipe it down with a

Defect	Cause	Remedy
1. Blistering of paint film	Moisture beneath the film	Strip down and repaint
2. Cloudy appearance on paint film	Surface is damp	Rub down, repaint when surface is thoroughly dry
3. Efflorescence (white furry deposit) forms on surface, pushes paint film off	Soluble salts crystallize	Remove deposit by vigorous brushing until no deposit and loose paint film remains, repaint; in some cases it may be advisable to use an oil primer or oil paint to prevent disturbing further salts in the wall with water
4. Flaking off of paint film	(a) Dirty surface or (b) Efflorescence or (c) Damp plaster	Strip down and repaint
5. Globules form, breaks appear in paint film	Surface is greasy, oily, or traces of turps on brush	Clean off grease, rub down and repaint
6. Gritty surface	Brush is dirty, dust has got into paint tin	Rub down and repaint
7. Pinholes appear in paint film	Over-vigorous stirring of paint, excessive brushing or moisture on the brush	Rub down and repaint
8. Ridges appear, brush marks are visible	Paint film applied too thickly or with too coarse a brush	Rub down and repaint

damp cloth to remove dirt and then paint over it. Wetting the wall-paper may affect its adhesion. As a precaution try a small patch first. This will show whether the wallpaper is adhering or not and whether it contains colours which may 'bleed' through.

The best treatment for old plaster surfaces that are pitted and crazed, but not drummy, is to fill the holes and line the whole surface with lining paper before painting. Drummy and perished plaster should be hacked off, of course, and the surface replastered.

Defects and remedies

Any number of reasons or combinations of reasons can cause defects in new paintwork. Some of the commoner causes of failure and their remedy are listed in the table below. In the long run two main causes are behind most failures. One is faulty or inadequate preparation; the other the presence of damp or moisture.

All new buildings collect a considerable quantity of water during construction. (The mixing of cement, concrete, plaster, and mortar all involve the use of water.) This water should be allowed to dry out before painting the surfaces, but if this is not possible then a paint or distemper should be used which will allow the surface to go on drying.

Old buildings, particularly basements, may suffer damp walls (see chapter 3). In such cases it is always worth while to try and find and then eradicate the cause of damp. In the long run it is cheaper and more effective to do this than to try to cover the damp with paint.

Efflorescence sometimes appears on the surface of external (and occasionally internal) brickwork. This occurs when moisture in the wall crystallizes soluble salts in the brickwork, forming a white, furry deposit on the surface. If the brickwork has been painted, the efflorescence will tend to push the paint film off the surface (see table of defects opposite).

Paperhanging

As with most jobs around the house success depends not only on using the right techniques but having the right tools.

The following should be regarded as a minimum.

T – G

Stripping knife. For removing old paint or wallpaper. See p. 183.

Filling knife. For applying filling to walls and ceilings.

Scissors. A large pair of ordinary scissors will do for cutting off the selvedge, trimming, etc., but paperhanger's scissors are available for the purpose. A 10-in. pair is the most useful size.

Paperhanger's brush. This has no handle but usually has hollows in the stock for holding. It is available in widths from 9 ins. to 12 ins. and is used for smoothing out the paper on the wall and pressing it into place.

Felt-covered roller. This is used for smoothing down the paper on the wall when an embossed wallpaper or one printed with distemper is used. A brush may damage the surface.

Seam roller. This is a small wooden roller used for rolling joints of paper after hanging.

Paste brush. A distemper brush (p. 182) is quite suitable for applying the paste to wallpaper.

In addition a large bucket for holding the paste, a sponge for mopping up excess paste from the skirting board and elsewhere, a folding 2-ft rule or a tape measure, and a plumb bob or large spirit level will be required. Professional paperhangers use a large board, known as a paste board, for applying the paste to the paper. Any large flat surface will do for this purpose but a paste board can be improvized with a sheet of hardboard, about 5 ft × 2 ft, strengthened with $1\frac{1}{2}$-in. × 1-in. timber battens screwed to the underside around the edges.

Paste

Paste for paperhanging can be mixed from flour and water. Mix 4 lb. of plain flour with about a quart of warm water and beat into a smooth creamy consistency; add a gallon of boiling water and stir until the mixture thickens into a heavy paste. Today there are a number of proprietary paste preparations on the market and, by following the manufacturer's instructions, it is easy to make a satisfactory paste.

Preparation of surfaces

Preparing wall and ceiling surfaces for wallpaper is much the same procedure as preparing them for paint. A previously painted plaster surface should be washed down with hot water and a mild detergent or sugar soap. It should then be rinsed with clean water and, whilst still wet, rubbed down with pumice stone or waterproof abrasive paper. Cracks should be filled with a proprietary filler and rubbed down to a finish flush with the surrounding surface. The surface should then be sized. The object of sizing is not so much to render the surface non-absorbent as to reduce its porosity and ensure that this condition is uniform all over the surface. Concentrated powder size, sold in packets and mixed with water according to the manufacturer's instructions, is brushed on to the surface using a flat distemper brush. Some cellulose paints also perform the function of sizing the surface.

If the wall or ceiling surface is already papered it is advisable to strip the old wallpaper. This may be done by soaking it with water, applied with an old distemper brush, leaving it for about twenty minutes to half an hour and then scraping it off with a stripping knife. In very old houses stripping the old wallpaper may expose drummy areas of plaster or even pull off the upper surface of the plaster in patches. Such drummy or defective areas should be hacked off and re-plastered. In the case of a lath and plaster surface consideration should be given to lining it with lining paper before applying wallpaper. Lining paper should be used under a heavy embossed wallpaper. In this case it is usual to hang the lining paper horizontally. Once the old wallpaper has been stripped cracks should be filled and rubbed down, the whole surface rinsed with clean water and lightly rubbed down and finally sized, all as described above.

Preparation of the wallpaper

Wallpaper has a selvedge, or plain edge along each side. Its purpose is to protect the ends of rolls during storage and transport and it must be removed before the paper is hung. Some suppliers will trim the selvedge, otherwise you can do it yourself. Scissors are suitable for this purpose but an alternative is to use a sharp knife and a straight edge.

The next step is to cut the paper to length. To do this the surfaces must be very carefully measured. Allow an extra 2 ins. (minimum) in the length for waste. Once the first length is measured and cut, it is normally satisfactory to use it as a guide in cutting the remaining lengths. An alternative practical method for measuring wall lengths is to take a roll and, starting at the skirting (allowing a 2 ins. overlap) unroll it up the wall, making a small tear at one side at the cornice or picture rail. It can then be cut off on the paste board to this length.

Pasting and hanging

Walls. Lay the paper face down on the paste board so that one side is level with the far edge of the paste board and the top end level with the right hand end of the paste board. Paste should be applied evenly and not too thickly, starting with the far edge and right hand end. When this is done slide the paper towards you so that the near side is level with the near edge of the paste board. Apply the paste to this section, making sure to draw the brush across the edge, *but not back*, as this will allow paste to get under and on to the face of the paper. Once the paste is applied to the top section of paper as described it must be carefully folded over and the whole length drawn up the paste board until the bottom end is level with the left hand edge of the paste board (fig. 58). The exposed lower section is pasted and folded over to meet the previous fold. The paper must be left to soak for a short time before hanging.

Experts advise that the papering of a wall should commence at the window and work around to the farthest corner of the room. Joints are less likely to show than if the hanging is done towards the light. If a patterned paper is used it is advisable to check with a plumb bob and line that the window frame is vertical. If it is not, a vertical line must be marked on the wall in pencil or coloured chalk 21 ins. from the frame. Take the first length of folded paper and, firmly holding the top edge, allow the paper to fall gently so that the top section unfolds. Adjust the top right hand edge against the wall, allowing a small overlap at the cornice or picture rail, and pass the paperhanging brush down the middle of the paper and from side to side. Crease the paper against the cornice or picture rail with the rounded end of the scissors, pull a short length away from the wall, trim off the waste, and then press it back to the wall. The lower half of the length should then be unfolded and fixed as described above. In hanging subsequent lengths care must be taken

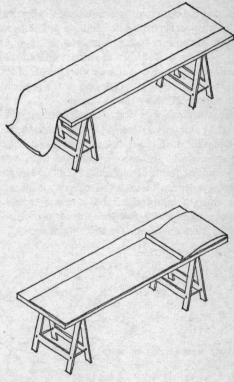

Fig. 58. Pasting and folding wallpaper

to butt the adjacent vertical joints accurately. When several lengths have been hung place a piece of paper over each joint in turn and run the roller over it. At corners the paper must be cut to width after pasting but before hanging, allowing about $\frac{1}{2}$ in. to turn the corner. At each corner it is necessary to check with the plumb bob and line and adjust the first length around the corner so that it is hanging vertically. At a chimney breast or other protrusion into the room it is advisable to paper the front face first. The sides should be hung afterwards so that they lap the part which has turned the corner.

Ceiling. Pasting the ceiling lengths follows the same procedure as that for the walls. The method of folding differs however. The paper should be folded concertina-fashion (fig. 59). Again start hanging at the window. Take up the pasted and folded first length of paper and support it over a spare roll or length of broomstick. Release the first fold and place the end of the paper in position against the cornice allowing the usual overlap. Once positioned, unfold more paper and brush it into place, brushing first down the centre and then along the edges. When the whole length has been unfolded and positioned the ends should be marked and trimmed as described for walls. As with papering the walls care must be exercised in butting joints of succeeding lengths. Needless to say, when papering a ceiling it is essential to have a firm scaffolding or support on which to stand and this should be long enough to enable you to move easily and safely from one side of the room to the other as you unfold and fix in position each length of paper.

Fig. 59. Folding paper for application to the ceiling

CHAPTER 15

Timber decay and infestation

Most houses contain a large quantity of timber. It is either rough surfaced (sawn) or smooth (planed). Generally sawn timber is not exposed to view. This includes most of the structural timbers, for example floor and ceiling joists, wall plates, rafters, and roof framing. Planed timber (sometimes referred to as *dressed*) is used for joinery work such as door frames, windows, picture rails, dado rails, skirtings, architraves, cupboards, and stairs.

Both sawn and planed timbers are susceptible to attack by fungi, which causes decay, and by insects. The more important insect damage is caused by the larvae (or 'worms') of wood-boring beetles and is recognized by the small exit holes in the timber, formed by the beetles when they emerge, and by the wood dust on or beneath the infested timber. The fungi which attack timber are plants belonging to the same group as toadstools and mushrooms. They decompose the wood and eventually leave it in a dry, friable state.

Fungal attack

The terms *wet rot* and *dry rot* are often loosely applied to timber attacked by fungi. Decay of timber may be caused by several different fungi. In most cases it is due either to the true dry rot fungus, *Merulius lacrymans*, or the Cellar Fungus, *Coniophora cerebella*, which only attacks wood which is definitely wet. The latter is often called wet rot.

Fungal attack develops actively only under moist conditions. Fungus is unable to grow in wood unless the moisture content is appreciably above 20 per cent. It often occurs, therefore, in external door frames near the ground and in window sills. In this case it is almost always the result of paint having peeled off or the *pointing* between window or door frame and wall having broken

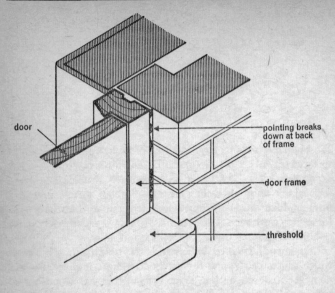

Fig. 60. Cause of rot to external door frames

down, permitting water to get in behind the frame (fig. 60). Fungal attack leading to timber decay occurs in unventilated parts of the building which have become damp: basements or under floors, for example.

Timber embedded in brickwork is particularly susceptible to fungal attack. Dampness in walls produces conditions in which fungus can flourish. Chapter 3 deals with causes of this. Throughout the house there are many hidden places where damp or rain penetration can occur. Timber in the vicinity is very likely to be affected if damp conditions are allowed to persist.

Timber which has been properly seasoned is safe from decay so long as it remains dry.

Prevention

There are four basic rules for preventing fungal attack:

1. Regularly inspect all woodwork, in particular the bottom of doors and door frames, window frames, the bottom sash of

windows, and window sills. Check the condition of the paintwork and the pointing.

2. Make sure that concealed timber is well ventilated. This means that air bricks in the walls below ground-floor level should be kept clear.

3. Make sure that timber unavoidably exposed to damp conditions is impregnated with preservative.

4. Do not paint damp or unseasoned timber. At best this results in premature failure of the paint film. At worst it keeps the wood in a moist condition for long enough to allow decay to develop.

Recognition. Fig. 1 chapter 1 illustrates the parts of a house where fungal attack is particularly likely to occur. If you suspect its presence, dig a knife blade or screwdriver into the wood. If it goes in and comes out easily, the wood is rotten. The true dry rot fungus (*Merulius lacrymans*) in an advanced stage grows a large fruiting body which has on it tiny spores. These are like a fine, reddish powder and may be visible on the woodwork. Look for waviness in skirtings, window linings, or picture rails. Dry rot has a characteristic smell, unlike mildew or mould, but most people cannot recognize it by its smell. Mould, of course, does not decay woodwork and can easily be brushed off. Its presence, however, does indicate dampness which may lead to dry rot.

Remedies

1. Remove and replace every piece of rotted wood, including about 12 ins. of sound timber on either side of the outbreak.

2. Thoroughly inspect the surrounding woodwork for further outbreaks.

3. In the case of decayed timber which is adjacent to or built into a wall the plaster should be hacked away in the vicinity to expose the full extent of the run of fungus strands between plaster and brickwork. These should be completely removed by brushing and scraping. Another method is to use a blowlamp, playing the flame on the exposed brickwork until it is quite hot. This method is not recommended, however, unless you are very experienced or employ a skilled man, as there is considerable risk of fire. The infected brickwork should then be 'painted' with sodium penta-

chlorophenate (8 oz. to a gallon of water) or a reliable ready-made solution.

4. Burn all infected wood right away. The fungus can spread if the infected wood is left lying about.

5. Find the cause of the dampness. It may be an obstructed air brick or a broken rainwater downpipe. It may be a leak in a water pipe or a damaged flashing. When you have found the cause put it right.

6. All new timber built into previously infected walls should be impregnated with preservative by a vacuum pressure method. If impregnated timber is not available the ends of joists and beams should be treated by standing them overnight in a preservative solution before building in.

7. Treat all sound timber in the vicinity of the attack with two coats of a proprietary preservative treatment brushed on.

Preservatives

One of the best preservatives is creosote. It should preferably be applied hot as it then penetrates more effectively. As a warning, however, timber treated with creosote is liable to 'bleed' into plaster or paintwork with which it comes into contact. There are several proprietary tar-oil preservatives on the market which are similar to creosote but have less smell. The use of oil tar preservatives should be avoided in rooms where food is stored as they may taint the food. If you want to paint woodwork after treatment it is necessary to use one of the solution type preservatives, a chemical dissolved either in water or in a special spirit solvent. Types are available which are colourless and therefore suitable for use on timber which is to have a clear finish.

Wood-boring insects

Most people are aware of the existence of wood-boring insects and of the damage they can cause. There are a number of species. Of these, the common furniture beetle is the most prevalent. It attacks the sapwood in timbers. Plywood made from birch or alder and bonded with animal glues is particularly susceptible.

Common Furniture Beetle (Anobium punctatum). This is the most frequent pest. Its popular name is misleading as it by no means confines its activities to furniture. Its life-cycle is in four stages – egg, larva, pupa, and adult. Eggs are laid in cracks and particularly in end grain. Rough surfaces on the underside or backs of furniture and the edges of plywood are popular egg-laying sites. Normally eggs hatch in four to five weeks and the larvae bore into the wood, forming tunnels which become loosely filled with dust. It is when this dust falls out of the holes that attack is often first apparent. When fully grown, the larva changes into a pupa and then, after six to eight weeks, into a beetle. Beetles bore through the wood forming circular 'flight' holes and emerge usually between the months of May and August. They may be seen, particularly on sunny days, crawling on walls and ceilings and flying about.

Lyctus Powder-post Beetles. This particular insect gets its name from the way in which its larva reduces timber to a fine powder. Its life-cycle from egg to beetle varies from 1 to 2 years and beetles emerge from late May to early in September. They are not active during the day but fly about at dusk, particularly in warm weather. They attack the sapwood of some hardwoods. They have been described as pests of timber yards and manufacturers' premises as this is where they most frequently occur, and it is only when actively infested timber is inadvertently used in the manufacture of joinery or furniture that the powder-post beetle finds its way into the house.

Death-watch Beetle (Xestobium rufovillosum). This insect prefers old timber which has become decayed either through lack of ventilation or because it was unseasoned when first used. It will not attack newly seasoned, sound timber. Eggs are deposited in cracks and crevices on the surface of the timber, in old tunnels and existing holes. They hatch in 2 to 8 weeks. The larvae then wander over the surface of the timber before boring in. When a larva is fully grown it changes into a pupa in July or August and 2 to 3 weeks later into a beetle, which remains within the timber until the following spring when it emerges through a round exit hole about $\frac{1}{8}$ in. in diameter.

House Longhorn Beetle (Hylotrupes bajulus). This species, unlike other members of the longhorn beetle family, which are essentially forest insects, attacks seasoned timber, affecting, however, softwoods only. It is rare in this country, however, except in parts of Surrey. As usual, eggs are laid in cracks and crevices. Larvae appear after about 2 weeks and bore into the timber. After feeding on the timber for several weeks (when the damage is done) it changes into a pupa and within 2 to 3 weeks into a beetle, emerging from the timber usually in July, August, and September, forming oval exit holes with a major diameter of $\frac{1}{4}$ to $\frac{3}{8}$ in.

Prevention

1. Inspect all timber in the house at least once a year. A good time to make the inspection is in summer during warm weather when the beetles are most likely to be active. It is important to look at timbers which are in relatively inaccessible positions, for this is just where insects will flourish. Roof timbers and under the ground-floor are favourite places. Do not forget unused articles of furniture stored in attics or basements.

2. Do not bring wood-boring insects into the house. Examine carefully all second-hand furniture you may buy and any timber brought into the house to be used for repairs or improvements.

3. Consider protecting inaccessible timber with a recognized wood preservative. There are a number of effective proprietary treatments on the market and details may be obtained from the Building Centre or the British Wood Preserving Association in London, or from the Scottish Building Centre in Glasgow. Remember, however, that the effectiveness of treatment depends upon the treated surface remaining intact. Subsequent splitting or cutting of the timber will expose untreated areas.

It is possible to have timber and plywood treated against fungal and insect attack during manufacture. The cost is not great. The British Wood Preserving Association will supply names of timber merchants who hold stocks.

Recognition

The presence of wood-boring insects will be apparent from bore

hole dust and flight holes in the timber. The existence of flight
holes alone does not necessarily mean that insects are active. They
may be old holes. Nor does it mean that your house is going to fall
down or your furniture collapse. Timber used structurally has a
fairly large margin of safety. But it is unwise to neglect attack.

The table below lists the identifying features of attack by various
insects and the timbers they go for. The Forest Products Research
Laboratory, which is a division of the Department of Scientific
and Industrial Research, has produced a number of leaflets on the
subject.

Insect	Timbers it attacks	Flight holes
Common furniture beetle	Seasoned hardwoods and softwoods. (Usually only sapwood) Plywood	Circular, approximately $\frac{1}{16}$ in. diameter
Lyctus powder-post beetles	Seasoned and partly seasoned hardwoods (Usually only sapwood but may emerge through heartwood)	As above
Death-watch beetle	Old, decayed hardwoods	Circular, approximately $\frac{1}{8}$ in. diameter
House longhorn beetle	Seasoned, sound softwoods (Usually only sapwood)	Oval, approximately $\frac{1}{4}$ in. $\times$ $\frac{1}{8}$ in.

In the event of extensive insect attack of the woodwork in a house,
whether of structural timbers or joinery or of furniture, advice is
available from the Forest Products Research Laboratory, the
Timber Research and Development Association, or the British
Wood Preserving Association. There are a number of specialist
firms throughout the country who undertake the work of eradicating infestation and applying preventative treatment. The methods
they use vary according to the type of insect attack, its extent, and
the conditions in the house.

Common furniture beetle. When attack is not severe treatment by insecticide will usually suffice. The full extent of the attack should be discovered by thorough examination. All powdery disintegrated surfaces should be removed and the remaining woodwork cleaned down. The insecticide should be applied by brush, or by dipping if this is practicable. When the timber is relatively inaccessible (the feet of rafters, for instance) it may be necessary to spray the insecticide on: builders' merchants sell spray outfits which are suitable for this purpose. A low pressure nozzle should be used as it gives a wider coverage. Particular attention should be given to cracks and crevices, to joints, to the underside of chairs, to the back of drawers, and similar positions, as this is just where the insect lays its eggs. In the case of furniture and panelling the effectiveness of treatment can be improved by injecting insecticide into the exit holes. Surface treatment reduces risk of re-infestation, but beetles emerging through treated surfaces will expose untreated timber beneath. Further applications of insecticide may be necessary. A number of proprietary preparations are available. Some of them contain the contact insecticides *benzene hexachloride* (BHC), DDT, and dieldrin.

When attack is widespread and severe, treatment should be carried out by specialist firms. They have special equipment for applying insecticide. An alternative treatment is fumigation with hydrogen cyanide or methyl bromide, a method which must be carried out by firms specializing in this form of treatment.

Lyctus powder-post beetles. Attack which is not severe may be treated in a similar way to attack by the common furniture beetle, although it is unlikely that a single application of insecticide would be sufficient to completely eradicate attack. Treatments by specialist firms include heat sterilization of infested furniture and fumigation with certain poisonous gases. Kiln-sterilization of new timber before it is used in house building is an effective method of eradicating attack but it does not prevent subsequent attack.

Death-watch beetle. This pest is most unlikely to attack timber in modern houses. Its favourite target is structural hardwood, particularly oak, in very old buildings. It goes for timber, such as built-in oak beams, in which penetration of moisture and lack of ventilation have led to decay. For this reason the first task is to remove the causes of fungal decay, which generally means removing the causes of damp penetration. Thereafter treatment with proprietary preparations should be carried out. Preparations include chemicals such as chlorinated naphthalenes, metallic naphthenates, polychlorophenols and their derivatives in penetrating solvents.

House longhorn beetle. Again, attack which is not severe can be treated as described for the common furniture beetle. Replacement timber should be treated with a wood preservative. Expert advice should be obtained in all cases of severe attack.

Conclusions

The presence of holes on the surface of timber does not necessarily call for action as the pest may no longer be active. There is no point in treating timber in this case, provided you are sure that the pest is extinct. One check is to look for dust created by the insect.

Not all insect attack is serious. The ambrosia beetle (pinhole borer), for example, attacks green timber only and dies out as soon as it dries. Another unimportant wood-boring insect is the *forest* longhorn beetle (as opposed to the *house* longhorn beetle). Neither of these insects is commonly found in houses.

Professional Institutions and Contractors' Organizations

Names and addresses of professional institutions and contractors' organizations concerned with the building industry are given at the end of this appendix.

Many of the maintenance and repair jobs described in this book are capable of being carried out by the amateur without professional guidance and advice. When expert advice is needed, however, consideration should be given to employing the services of an architect. An architect's job is to design buildings but his professional training also fits him to advise on such detailed matters as the structural stability of a house, methods of sound-proofing a building and of providing thermal insulation, and the planning of house alterations and additions. Many people do not realize this; nor are they aware that the fees charged for such work are not high and that some architects actually specialize in this type of work. Names and addresses of architects and information concerning the nature of the services an architect will provide and the fees he will charge can be obtained from the Secretary of the Royal Institute of British Architects.

In certain circumstances the services of a surveyor may be required. For instance, when contemplating purchasing a house, a thorough survey by an independent professional surveyor is a wise safeguard. Inquiries concerning the employment of a surveyor should be directed to the Secretary of the Royal Institution of Chartered Surveyors.

Professional advice may also be obtained on the installation of central heating. Generally, however, it is satisfactory to go direct to a reputable contractor. If you require professional advice write to the Secretary of the Institution of Heating and Ventilating

Engineers. For names and addresses of contractors contact the Secretary of the Heating and Ventilating Contractors' Association.

For those jobs which are too ambitious for the amateur, such as extensive repairs, structural alterations and additions, the services of a reputable builder will be required. If an architect is employed he will normally act for you in selecting and instructing a builder. Otherwise you should obtain the names and addresses of builders specializing in this type of work in your district from the Secretary of the National Federation of Building Trades Employers. He may redirect your inquiry to one of the many regional offices of the bodies making up the Federation.

For names and addresses of plumbers and roofing contractors write to the Secretary of the appropriate Association. Addresses are given below:

Royal Institute of British Architects,
66 Portland Place, London W1

Royal Institution of Chartered Surveyors,
12 Great George Street, Parliament Square,
Westminster, London SW1

Institution of Heating and Ventilating Engineers,
49 Cadogan Square, London SW1

National Federation of Building Trades Employers,
82 New Cavendish Street, London W1

Heating and Ventilating Contractors' Association,
172 Buckingham Palace Road, London SW1

Registered Plumbers' Association,
Hamilton House, 285 Romford Road,
Forest Gate, London E7

The National Federation of Roofing Contractors,
West Bar Chambers, 38 Boar Lane, Leeds 1

Technical Information and Advisory Organizations

There is no lack of reliable technical information available to the public: the problem is knowing where to find what you want. This appendix lists a number of organizations whose function includes the dissemination of information on subjects related to house building, house maintenance and repairs, household appliances and equipment.

British Electrical Development Association, 2 Savoy Hill, London WC2, is an organization representing the electricity supply industry of the United Kingdom: membership includes supply undertakings in other countries. Its principal aim is to promote the wider and more efficient use of electricity. It maintains testing laboratories and publishes technical information. There is a permanent exhibition and information centre at The Building Centre, London.

British Standards Institution, 2 Park Street, London W1, is an independent organization financed in part by subscriptions from its members, in part from the sale of standards and other publications, and in part by a Government grant. Membership is open to any British subject or to any body duly constituted in any part of the British Commonwealth. Its primary function is to produce standards covering agreed constructional, operational, or technological requirements of a product or process. Standards fall into five major categories: dimensional standards, performance or quality standards, standard methods of test, standards covering technical terms, and symbols and standard codes of practice. The latter set out the most efficient method of installation, use, and maintenance of equipment and recommend methods for technical operations. Standards are prepared by committees drawn from all ranks of industry and technology and are issued only when there is agreement amongst producers, distributors, and users of the product concerned. Members of B.S.I. purchase standards and other publications at a discount of 10 per cent, and receive the monthly magazine 'B.S.I. News' and 'British Standards Year-book' which contains brief abstracts of some 3,500 published standards and a complete subject index.

British Wood Preserving Association, 6 Southampton Place, London WC1, is an organization which collects information on the preservation and fireproofing of timber and on methods of apply-ing preservatives and fire retardants. It sponsors scientific research into the use of preservatives and fire retardants and makes available the results of its research through the publication of leaflets, a technical advice service, and specialist lectures.

The Building Centre, 26 Store Street, London WC1, maintains a permanent exhibition of building materials and products backed by a comprehensive information service. Inquiries can be made in person, by telephone, or by letter. The Centre is organized prim-arily for those professionally concerned with building, but the service is also available to the public. Exhibitor's information sheets can be supplied.

Similar Centres exist in major cities throughout the country, at the following addresses:

BIRMINGHAM   The Engineering and Building Centre,
              Broad Street, Birmingham 1

BRISTOL   Bristol Building Centre Limited,
              Stonebridge House, Colston Avenue, Bristol 1

CAMBRIDGE   The Building Information Centre,
              16 Trumpington Street, Cambridge

GLASGOW   The Scottish Building Centre,
              425–7 Sauchiehall Street, Glasgow C2

MANCHESTER   The Manchester Building Centre,
              113–15 Portland Street, Manchester 1

NOTTINGHAM   Midland Design and Building Centre,
Mansfield Road, Nottingham.

Cement and Concrete Association, 52 Grosvenor Gardens, London
SW1, is an independent non-profit making organization, the
membership of which is open to all cement manufacturers in
Great Britain and Northern Ireland. It is financed from a voluntary
self-imposed levy paid by member companies. Its aim is to advise
on and promote the intelligent use of cement and concrete. The
C.C.A. maintains research laboratories and a technical library, and
publishes technical literature, amongst which is a series of do-it-
yourself booklets, available free from the Association. It also runs
a technical advice service: inquiries are normally answered by
letter.

Coal Utilization Council, 19 Rochester Row, London SW1, is a
national organization supported by the producers and distributors
of solid fuels and by the manufacturers and distributors of the
domestic heating and cooking appliances which use them. It aims
to promote wider and more efficient use of coal, coke, and other
solid fuels. Through its Information Centres in London and major
cities throughout the country, the Council is able to offer technical
advice to the public on solid fuel heating and cooking. The
Council's Information Centre at The Building Centre, London,
contains a permanent exhibition of solid fuel appliances and
equipment. Addresses of regional Information Centres are:

BIRMINGHAM   93–7 John Bright Street, Birmingham

BRISTOL   39 Park Street, Bristol

CAMBRIDGE   24 St Andrew's Street, Cambridge

CARDIFF   69–70 St Mary Street, Cardiff

EDINBURGH   9 Atholl Place, Edinburgh 3

GLASGOW   341 Bath Street, Glasgow C2

LEEDS   9 Wellington Street, City Square, Leeds 1

MANCHESTER   4 Barton Arcade, Deansgate, Manchester 3

NEWCASTLE-
UPON-TYNE   18 Saville Row, Newcastle-upon-Tyne 1

Nottingham   4 and 6 St Peter's Gate, Nottingham

Plymouth   Royal Cinema Building, Athenaeum Place,
              Plymouth

The Council produces numerous leaflets and publications which are available to the public and, in addition, a list of approved solid fuel appliances. Appliance distributors, who satisfy certain conditions imposed by the C.U.C. concerning the service they provide to the public, are entitled to describe themselves officially as C.U.C. Approved Appliance Distributors and this represents a safeguard to the public. Similar schemes are operated by the C.U.C. to cover Approved Coal Merchants and Approved Appliance Fixers. The C.U.C. supports the Women's Advisory Council on Solid Fuel (18 South Molton Street, London W1) which is concerned with promoting and advising on efficient heating by solid fuels among the leading national women's organizations and housewives generally.

Consumers' Association, 14 Buckingham Street, London WC2, is an independent organization which carries out tests on consumer goods bought across the counter in the normal way and publishes the results in its monthly journal *Which?* Anyone can join C.A. but no member of its governing body may be engaged in industry, commerce, or advertising. Its sole income is the money obtained from the sale of publications and the fees of its members: it receives no money from the State or from industry or commerce.

The Design Centre, 28 Haymarket, London SW1, is a permanent exhibition of well designed modern British consumer goods. It is organized by The Council of Industrial Design, a government-sponsored body, the purpose of which is to foster the improvement of standards of design in the products of British industry.

The Design Centre maintains a Design Index, which is a detailed record in the form of photographs and samples of nearly 10,000 well designed goods. Products represented in the Index range from wall tiles to washing machines, from door knobs to dishes. By consulting the Design Index members of the public will be directed immediately to those products which represent the highest standards of design.

Gas Council, 1 Grosvenor Place, London SW1, is the organization established when the gas industry was nationalized in 1949. Its primary aims are to advise the Minister of Power on matters concerning the industry and to assist the Area Gas Boards in the efficient performance of their functions. Generally it is the local Gas Board to whom inquiries should be directed in the first place for advice on gas as a fuel and on the use of gas appliances. But the Gas Council produces numerous publications of interest to the public.

The Heating Centre, 34 Mortimer Street, London W1, exhibits heating appliances and equipment and there is a staff in attendance which will answer technical inquiries from the public. Inquiries can be made in person, by telephone, or by letter. The Heating Centre exists to promote house heating and hence serves the interests of the heating manufacturing and contracting industries. However, its advice to the public is impartial and hence useful in distinguishing the sometimes conflicting claims of the various fuel interests.

Rural Industries Bureau, 35 Camp Road, Wimbledon Common, London SW19, is an organization financed by Treasury grants from the Development Fund to encourage and develop rural industries. Thus information can be obtained on such rural building techniques as roof thatching and the Bureau will supply members of the public, on inquiry, with names of thatchers operating in their district.

Timber Research and Development Association, maintains an information centre and permanent exhibition at The Building Centre, London. It is an independent research organization, financed jointly by the Timber Trades Federation of the United Kingdom, the Department of Scientific and Industrial Research, and member firms and individuals in all branches of industry. Its purpose is to advise on and promote the intelligent use of timber. In addition to its exhibition at The Building Centre it maintains research laboratories and publishes technical literature concerning timbers and their applications.

Other trade development associations which provide technical information and publish informative literature include:

The Aluminium Development Association,
33 Grosvenor Street, London W 1

The Copper Development Association,
55 South Audley Street, London W 1

The Lead Development Association,
34 Berkeley Square, London W 1

The Zinc Development Association,
34 Berkeley Square, London W 1

Government Research Organizations
Government research organizations whose activities cover the
subject dealt with in this book include:

The Building Research Station

The Forest Products Research Laboratory

The Joint Fire Research Organization

These organizations publish digests, reports, and other informative literature which are available from Her Majesty's Stationery
Office.

Glossary of technical terms

The terms used in this book have the following meanings:

aggregate One of the basic ingredients of concrete, the other being cement.

box gutter Gutter between two sections or levels of roof or between roof and abutting wall.

building paper A tough paper, usually bitumen-impregnated, used in certain circumstances as an insulating barrier.

built-up roofing Several layers of material, usually organic fibre, asbestos-based, or glass fibre felt laid in hot bitumen to form a complete roof covering.

chamfer Cutting off of the edge of a piece of timber to an angle of 45°.

chase Groove cut in brick or concrete wall or ceiling surface to enable pipes, cables, etc. to be concealed.

clout A type of galvanized flat-headed nail used for fixing plasterboard.

coping Capping on top of a wall, fence, parapet, etc.

cutting in A term used by painters to describe fine work such as painting the edge of sashes abutting the glass line.

decking Continuous surface applied to the top of a roof, whether flat or pitched, usually in the form of timber boarding.

drummy When referring to plaster, means an area of plaster which has lost its adhesion to the wall.

expansion joint Joint formed in concrete or brickwork to take up the natural movement of the material.

flashing Strip of material, usually metal, fixed at the junction of two surfaces such as roof and chimney to prevent the penetration of rainwater.

flaunching Cement render applied to the top of a chimney to protect the brickwork. Forms a sloping surface to shed rainwater.

fletton A type of brick.

gauge As used in roof tiling, means the distance apart that tiling battens are placed.

grout A thin, fluid mortar used to fill joints in brickwork, stonework, or concrete where strength is not important.

hip The external angle formed by two inclined sides of a roof.

pointing The filling up of the joints in brickwork after the bricks have been laid.

quadrant Piece of timber, of small cross section, the profile of which is a quarter of a circle.

render A surface finish applied to brickwork with a trowel and composed of cement and sand and a small proportion of lime. The first coat of plaster on a masonry wall.

ridge The top of a roof where it rises to an acute angle.

size As used in paper hanging, a gelatinous solution applied to a surface before the paste. Its purpose is to reduce the porosity of a surface and ensure that a uniform condition is obtained over the whole surface. Some cellulose pastes also serve the function of sizing the surface.

space heating Term used to describe the heating of a whole room or space.

spalling The breaking down or decomposition of the exposed surface of brickwork or stonework.

soffit The underside of a balcony, overhanging eaves, etc.

soil pipe Pipe which carries discharge from w.c. to sewer.

stop cock Mechanism for shutting off the flow of water in a pipe. Usually has a handle like a tap. Sometimes called a stopvalve.

template A pattern or guide, often in the form of a piece of timber or building board or sheet metal.

valley The internal angle formed by two inclined sides of a roof.

waste pipe Pipe which carries discharge from sink, basin, and bath to sewer.

*

A full glossary of technical terms is contained in *A Dictionary of Building* by John S. Scott, Penguin Reference Books R15.

Index